CALVIN J. KING

The Christian Nurture of Youth

A Guide for Leaders of Youth

The Christian
Nurture of Youth

Ada Zimmerman Brunk
Ethel Yake Metzler

Herald Press, Scottdale, Pennsylvania

Contents

Introduction

Wise investments in youth yield eternal dividends. The potential of young people in the church is beyond the measure of human calculations. To lose them is fatal to the Christian community. They are needed for leadership in spirituality, for stewardship of possessions, for vision of opportunity, for courage to undertake the difficult tasks, and for moral and financial support of the total Christian enterprise. They are the most significant segment of people in the church. But we are constantly confronted with the questions: "How can we conserve them? How can we train them? How can we involve them in the life and work of the church?"

The church's work with youth is essentially a matter of guidance to help them achieve maturity. From awaking childhood to settled adulthood, they pass through periods of growth and stages of development. To be helpful through these years requires understanding and patience. The first chapter of this book outlines the resources adults need to work with young people. The youth leader must take heed to himself and to the teachings of Scripture to qualify for his position of leadership.

Beyond knowing one's self is the challenge of knowing youth. The authors of this book have not only lived close to youth, but they have been serious students of youth potential and reaction. They have shared with the reader significant insights and valid judgments about the propensities of youth and about what to do with them. Instead of giving dogmatic advice on how to do it, they have suggested causes of youth reaction, the symptoms of basic need, and possible ways in which these needs can be met. They stimulate desire to be helpful in right ways and provide criteria by which to judge the effectiveness of youth activities.

In the last chapter of this book the reader is introduced to basic principles of guidance. The counselor of youth will find here a variety of practical methods of approach and a wealth of source materials well suited to the needs of young people. It is particularly helpful in learning how to think problems through to valid conclusions, in vocational guidance, and in promoting conviction for service in the church.

Ada Zimmerman Brunk was for many years a teacher of psychology at Eastern Mennonite College. She served also as a personnel dean. In both positions she performed the role of counselor with ease, understanding, and effectiveness. Her rich experience with young people, her own vital Christian discipleship, her broad academic training, and her deep devotion to youth and the church qualified her well for the writing of this book. Much of the material was prepared under the handicap of pain and physical weakness resulting from her fatal illness. At her death the manuscript was unfinished.

Ethel Yake Metzler represents the succeeding generation. She has served significantly in youth activities, in preparing materials for youth groups, and in direct youth leadership. These experiences developed in her qualities of insight and judgments that qualified her very well to edit and revise the materials left by Mrs. Brunk. She brought together the vital materials, added parts of her own composition, and organized the chapters in the book.

These two authors make a happy combination of matured wisdom and contemporary sensitivity. The whole message is framed in an orientation of Christian faith related to psychological principles. It is deeply rooted in loyalties and objectives that promote the lordship of Christ in the life of youth today.

John R. Mumaw

Chapter 1

Working with Young People

IF YOU have ever stood before a class of teen-agers who seem to mirror each other, looking as much alike as the latest models of cars, you've probably had that awesome feeling of being on the outside—looking on, not in, wondering what role you are to play in this one-way street where teen-agers seem to be going the wrong way. You've had that uncomfortableness of questions plaguing your subconscious. Who are these adolescents? What makes them the way they are? What am I to them? How can I be any help to them on their way to maturity? How?

These feelings put you in good company. For teen-agers have always perplexed and alarmed outsiders. And adults are always outside. That is part of the phenomenon of adolescence. Although adolescents thus seem to escape confinement and domestication, adolescence may be charted, described, and understood.

Parents try to manage teen-agers' money, time, and behavior. Educators ladle out knowledge for them.

Sunday-school teachers apply platitudes and morals to their crazy-patch world. Merchants cater to their fads and fancies, advertisers chant jingles hoping they will catch with the teen crowd. Hollywood parades its glamour, entertainers beat out the rock and roll—or whatever is current, and religionists criticize and judge. All with varying degrees of success. What of counselors? How can you, a would-be leader, get going with youth? How can you help them steer a steady course from childhood to becoming an adult?

First, you must know yourself. You must know that you have encountered God and accepted Jesus Christ as your Saviour. You must be certain that you desire to do God's will above all else. This knowledge is indispensable if you would guide adolescents. Their understandings of salvation are beginning to be tested by the experiences of arriving at independence and achieving freedom to do as they choose. They can respect a leader whose life demonstrates how acceptance of Christ as his Saviour affects behavior.

Adolescents despise sham and pretense. Sincerity, humility, and consistency rate high in their evaluation, and they have an uncanny way of discovering hypocrisy.

Furthermore, awareness that you are committed to God and His will, will motivate you to seek His presence, to rely on His power, and to discover His will through reading the Bible.

A leader is always in danger of wearing his soul thin with constant activity. Rushing around, doing worthwhile things may leave him exhausted and irritable at the close of the day. Then, when he would pray, he discovers that God seems far away, for he has left Him out of his thoughts, planning, and activity all through the day. A leader dare not substitute bluster, noise, organization, nor activity for the search for God's glory and will.

You must accept the challenge of your capacity for growth. Teen-agers respect a person who knows more than they, but who refrains from giving his opinions on matters of opinion until he is asked. Research has pushed back the frontiers of science. Communications and ease of travel have shrunk our world. Teen-agers study history, science, social geography, and current events. In these matters they may have as up-to-date facts as their leader. But in the areas of Christianity and Bible knowledge, and personal and interpersonal relationships they are just learning. The leader who accepts the confidence and recognition teen-agers place in him as a challenge to improve himself and his relations with other people will find his growth in mind and spirit the finest service to those he would lead.

To acquire Bible knowledge a leader must aggressively pursue a definite program of study. Haphazard reading cannot insure results either in broader understandings, accumulation and relating of facts to each other, or deeper spiritual perceptions. Only active study, accepted as a responsibility, can open up the Scriptures. This is a resource a Christian who would lead youth cannot afford to pass by. A minimum of books to aid in your understanding of the Bible should include a Bible dictionary, atlas, geography, and one or more commentaries.

Growth is also essential to your Christian experience. Men of all ages who have inspired others to faith have practiced the presence of God. They have been men of devotion and fellowship, who have yielded their leadership to the superior leadership of the Holy Spirit. This is an ongoing process, for one day's achievement does not suffice for the next. Each day offers new opportunities for discipline and growth Godward.

A person thus committed to a life of righteousness can test his growth toward maximum Christian living by asking himself each day, questions in the following list. A progressively improved score will indicate growth spurred by intensive purpose.

Today:

1. Did I thank the Lord for the privilege of being His and experiencing freedom from past sin?

2. Did I find a nugget of truth in the Bible that left a challenging impression with me all day?

3. Was I conscious of God's presence whatever my task?

4. Did I refrain from foolish and idle talk?

5. Did I gain a victory over some immaturity? And as a result feel a dynamic pulse of power?

6. Did I ask God's forgiveness for a wrong I permitted in an unguarded moment?

7. Did I exchange at least one spiritual truth with someone?

8. Did I ask for one definite thing in prayer?

9. Did God answer at least one request that I made today or during the past week?

10. Did I pray for at least one unsaved soul or some-

one who needs to discover the joys of discipleship?

11. Have I been so nearly one with Him that at a moment's notice I can carry out a commission He might give me?

12. Did I reaffirm my consecration to God?

When you can say "yes" to most of these questions, you are living the inner life that supports an aggressive spiritual leadership. Young people are quick to recognize a leader whose inner strength produces outward poise. Such a person, on good terms with himself because he is learning from his experiences, who respects himself and offers that same respect to others, is in a position to help young people.

Second, you must know teen-agers. You must be aware of what they expect a good leader to be. Here is a list compiled from answers of several hundred young people to the question: What qualities do you desire in your spiritual leader?

1. He must be genuinely Christian, know the Bible, practice what he preaches, and be interested in the salvation of others.

2. He must like us, be friendly, remember names and faces, and make us feel free to come with our problems.

3. He must fit in with young people, not be bossy, have a sense of humor and be ready to learn from others.

4. He must be neat in appearance and be able to speak in public.

5. He must have an understanding and forgiving spirit (for there must be much that to him would not seem right).

Such a sympathetic leader, who can listen with unbiased opinion, appeals to youth. His power lies not in his skill to perform but in his ability to influence, to create desire, to stir motive, and to guide action. Adolescents resist authority and superiority. But the adult who accepts them as persons and not as problems, who shares their experiences, who likes them for what they are and not for what he would like to see them be, who believes that they can accept responsibility—to that person they will give respect. They will seek his counsel and accept his guidance.

To become this sort of understanding person you need also to know how adolescents grow and think and feel. You need to know to what kind of guidance they will respond and how. You need to know in what they are interested and how to help them discover answers to their questions about life. You need to learn to spot their concerns, to mirror their feelings, to sense the direction they are going or want to go, and with creativity draw upon your resources to show them the way.

This book seeks to show that adolescence is a normal growth process and to point up the viewpoint of this age group that takes refuge in a world of its own, that has come out from childhood's protection and is not yet admitted to adult freedom. It seeks also to point you, a leader of youth, to techniques for helping youth to choose the finest principles of thought and action and to apply them to their world. Further, it gives techniques for helping them to recognize and shoulder their responsibilities with initiative and their own innate capacities, thus developing self-confidence as they mature from self-interest to world-interest.

Chapter 2

Early Adolescence
Years 12 to 14

No SUDDEN changes mark the beginning and closing of this period when the child is no longer child, nor yet an adult. The time set by nature when each individual is first capable of reproducing his kind is not known, for puberty differs from person to person and with climate and race. But in temperate climates girls may become pubescent as early as eleven and as late as sixteen, and boys between thirteen and fifteen. Adolescence, or this period of transition, continues through the teens and reaches into the middle twenties.

Early adolescence, involving the years from twelve to fourteen, really reaches back several years to age ten when there is a marked slowing down of the steady growth progress the child has been making since birth. It is as though the body is mustering its forces for the pubertal spurt in growth that gradually progresses toward maturity. Middle adolescence usually involves

2

the years fifteen to seventeen, and later adolescence, or mature youth, from eighteen to twenty-four. Corresponding school divisions are: early adolescence, junior high school; middle adolescence, senior high school; later adolescence, college.

Although no sudden changes mark the beginning of adolescence, the changes are many, and they are there to be seen and interpreted. They concern everything about the child—making him act different, look different, and feel different. The way he feels and acts toward others will change, as does his attitude toward himself. Junior-intermediate leaders wonder what has gotten into Johnny—the way he giggles and is so self-conscious. And why does Marie, who was always so active and interested, seem so infuriatingly lazy, they wonder. A question catches Pete daydreaming. And Tom unexpectedly shows self-control when Harold tries to trip him.

Parents, too, notice changes. Their child, who seemed reasonably self-controlled, bursts into tears when they object to a plan she proposes. Arnold polishes his shoes without having to be reminded. Cliff makes a decision for the right that only a few months before he would have haggled over with his Dad. And Gladys unexpectedly shoulders taking care of the home when Mother is called away to nurse a sick relative.

Youth leaders can learn to recognize the signs of change and read them, not for what they appear to be on the surface but for what they suggest is going on in the minds and spirits of these boys and girls who are moving from childhood toward maturity.

Physical Changes

The pituitary gland at the base of the brain throws the switch that gets puberty under way. Its hormones activate the hormone secretions within the ovaries and testes and start the physical changes which forever sever youth from childhood.

The growth spurt comes first. The average girl, who has been shorter than the boy during childhood, becomes taller and gradually heavier between ages eleven and fourteen. After that she is permanently surpassed by the boy. Boys gain in height and weight between twelve and one half and fourteen, often shooting up within a year to the height of their fathers. The bony growth of the arms and legs is out of proportion to their muscle growth. Feet and hands are suddenly all out of proportion to the rest of the body. The development of the heart and lungs and muscles takes place over a period of considerable time. Boys and girls may react violently to this sudden change in size. Martha constantly walks with a slump to avoid looking taller than the rest of her grade. Tim refuses to go to Sunday school because his shoes pinch. He feared to ask for new ones because the last purchase had occasioned an increase of two sizes. He hated the clerk and his father for commenting on his shoe size.

Growth in size of the brain ceases in this early adolescent period, though cell development, upon which mental functioning depends, continues for many years. The heart develops more rapidly than the blood vessels, and this may result in a harmless palpitation or skipped beat that annoys some early teeners. Sweat glands also become more active, as do the sebaceous or oil glands that supply the skin and hair. This is one factor of the acne or skin blemish that troubles girls and boys in their teens.

Girls begin to menstruate during the period, although a few may begin earlier and a few later. Periods may be irregular, for early menstruation does not necessarily mean the girl is sexually mature in the sense of ovulating or being able to bear a child. A regular period for menses may not be established for more than a year, and then irregularities are often normal.

The appearance of pubic, underarm, and facial hair is usually considered as a mark of a boy's having passed into adolescence. The largest group of boys reaches puberty between ages fourteen and fifteen. Nocturnal emissions are a sign that the boy is maturing, for the semen that has been developing is thereby discharged.

A boy's voice change does not usually come before he is fifteen, after his growth spurt and physical changes have started to develop. A girl's voice also becomes richer and fuller as she moves into middle adolescence.

And their appetites are tremendous—so much so that a girl sometimes puts herself on a diet, not realizing that the filling out she has lately acquired will gradually ease into the proportions she desires. Although they consume enormous quantities of food, and their energy seems abundant, at times adolescents are listless and lazy. For all their size, they are not as strong as they look. Those late-lying-abed and poking-around times are ways of replenishing the energy they so readily exhaust.

EMOTIONAL GROWTH

To many adults there seems to be little rhyme or reason to the adolescent's business of living. His emotions well up like a flood—strong, and sometimes difficult to control. A minimum of stimuli produces a maximum of reactions. The mildest joke may make him laugh hilariously, and the least criticism may make him blazing mad or start a cloudburst of tears. Sudden outbursts of emotion often come as a surprise both to parents and teen-agers. Frequently, because parents sometimes misunderstand this change of reactions, they may tease, ridicule, or punish unwisely.

Adolescents themselves wonder why they feel highly elated, joyous, warmly sympathetic, and generously kind at one moment and then upon the slightest provocation —or for no reason at all—suddenly turn callous, bitter, sarcastic, or even cruel. Depressed, a boy may grow morose and morbid, a girl tearful, secretive, and brooding. Girls giggle and laugh when circumstances call for sober respect. A stimulus demands immediate action— and their actions are not always in keeping with their knowledge of correct and incorrect behavior—their knowledge of right and wrong. They act—then think. When the matter is lived in retrospect, they may discover that another response would have brought better results. Regretful and guilty, they chide themselves or justify their actions, or push into their unconscious minds these failures, disappointments, and limitations. Generally, the more forceful the personality, the more storm and stress is occasioned in the process of growing up.

Adults and leaders of young people can learn how to be helpful at this stage of emotional growth. Keeping alert for the specific causes of moods and depressions of a group will give a leader clues to the behavior puzzle. An important ball game coming up can have a definitely stimulating effect upon a group's emotions. Losing that ball game can reverse those feelings. During a Christian service activity, revival, or camp experience, they may maintain a prolonged state of elation and exaltation, only to plunge headlong into a depression, as fatigue sets in. Directors of youth camp programs hazard the total good of their program when they crowd the days and evenings with strenuous activities that exhaust youth's energies. An anticlimax of depression and defeat may be worse than never having had the tremendous uplifting experiences that, in the end, left them exhausted and fatigued. Adolescents are just beginning to estimate their own true value and feelings —and moodiness and elation often arise because of their inability to sense what is happening to them.

An adolescent's appearance may be the cause of recurring gloomy moods. Just when he is becoming conscious of his appearance, his features are changing— growing at different rates—and he may be keenly sensitive because of a large nose, chin, or forehead. Boys and girls of early adolescence need the reassurance that they will outlive most of the irregularities of growth. Fatness, tallness, a squeaky voice, littleness, overgrownness, unruly hair, a protruding Adam's apple, freckles, or prominent ears will no doubt be left behind with the years. And if his good features can be played up, the adolescent may forget the disturbing handicaps. Praise for attractive features of an adolescent's appearance may well be in order.

Youth want adventure, excitement. Around them they often find only dull routine. If they have anticipated some party, trip, or date—only to be disappointed —they can become moody and despondent, unless some alternate activity is substituted. A youth leader should be on his toes for such occasions and for these situations when Christian youth feel left out of school activities because of religious scruples. Then he can be prepared to initiate or stimulate interest in a project that will absorb their attention at the time they most need it. Belonging is a must for adolescents, and being left out— even if it is of their own volition—is disappointing and discouraging.

A leader can help adolescents refuse to be discouraged or defeated, by helping them discover meaning in Scripture verses. Go on they must—and the going is easier with chins up. A list might include these from both the Old and New Testaments:

Thou wilt keep him in perfect peace, whose mind is stayed on thee: because he trusteth in thee.—Isaiah 26:3.

And thine ears shall hear a word behind thee, saying, This is the way, walk ye in it, when ye turn to the right hand, and when ye turn to the left.—Isaiah 30:21.

For I the Lord thy God will hold thy right hand, saying unto thee, Fear not; I will help thee.—Isaiah 41:13.

I, even I, am he that blotteth out thy transgressions for mine own sake, and will not remember thy sins.— Isaiah 43:25.

And ye shall seek me, and find me, when ye shall search for me with all your heart.—Jeremiah 29:13.

Be of good courage, and he shall strengthen your heart, all ye that hope in the Lord.—Psalm 31:24.

Why art thou cast down, O my soul? and why art thou disquieted in me? hope thou in God.—Psalm 42:5.

Trust in the Lord with all thine heart; and lean not unto thine own understanding.—Proverbs 3:5.

He that is slow to anger is better than the mighty; and he that ruleth his spirit than he that taketh a city.—Proverbs 16:32.

Blessed are they which do hunger and thirst after righteousness: for they shall be filled.—Matthew 5:6.

But seek ye first the kingdom of God, and his righteousness; and all these things shall be added unto you.—Matthew 6:33.

For whosoever will save his life shall lose it: and whosoever will lose his life for my sake shall find it.—Matthew 16:25.

Let not your heart be troubled: ye believe in God, believe also in me.—John 14:1.

If ye abide in me, and my words abide in you, ye shall ask what ye will, and it shall be done unto you.—John 15:7.

And we know that all things work together for good to them that love God, to them who are the called according to his purpose.—Romans 8:28.

I am crucified with Christ: nevertheless I live; yet not I, but Christ liveth in me: and the life which I now live in the flesh I live by the faith of the Son of God, who loved me, and gave himself for me.—Galatians 2:20.

There hath no temptation taken you but such as is common to man: but God is faithful, who will not suffer you to be tempted above that ye are able; but will with the temptation also make a way to escape, that ye may be able to bear it.—I Corinthians 10:13.

Charity suffereth long, and is kind; charity envieth not; charity vaunteth not itself, is not puffed up, doth not behave itself unseemly, seeketh not her own, is not easily provoked, thinketh no evil.—I Corinthians 13:4, 5.

Be careful for nothing; but in every thing by prayer and supplication with thanksgiving let your requests be made known unto God. And the peace of God, which passeth all understanding, shall keep your hearts and minds through Christ Jesus.—Philippians 4:6, 7.

Finally, brethren, whatsoever things are true, whatsoever things are honest, whatsoever things are just, whatsoever things are pure, whatsoever things are lovely, whatsoever things are of good report; if there be any virtue, and if there be any praise, think on these things. Those things, which ye have both learned, and received, and heard, and seen in me, do.—Philippians 4:8, 9.

I can do all things through Christ which strengtheneth me.—Philippians 4:13.

For God hath not given us the spirit of fear; but of power, and of love, and of a sound mind.—II Timothy 1:7.

If we confess our sins, he is faithful and just to forgive us our sins, and to cleanse us from all unrighteousness.—I John 1:9.

Let every man be swift to hear, slow to speak, slow to wrath.—James 1:19.

INDULGING IN SELF-PITY

Self-pity is a habit many adolescents fall into when they feel they are not understood and cannot talk things over with their parents. Desire for adult freedom and inability to use it wisely are frequently causes for self-pity. When boys are thwarted in their desire to make decisions and to find their own standard of values, they often dream of—or even try—running away from home. Loud and angry words, slamming of doors, talking back, and mumbling behind their parents' backs are typical demonstrations of anger reactions to restraint. "Why does the family think they have to raise me?" one boy objected. "Couldn't a fellow just live with his folks?"

A girl is more likely to react by planning her own funeral, when she is in conflict with her mother over chores, taste, dress, etc. If she feels that she is not appreciated, or that too many tasks fall to her, or if family finances or conservative viewpoints make her parents restrain her from following the fads her clique establishes, a girl is likely to pity herself.

Self-pity is common in adolescents whose feelings are easily hurt, or in those who feel that they are carrying everybody's load and that no one appreciates what they do. It may be caused by a desire for freedom when it cannot be given them because of their inexperience, or from having to carry responsibility when they would prefer to be dependent. It may grow out of feelings of inferiority, and develop into the martyr feelings of some adults who consider themselves suffering heroes subjected to wrongs imposed by others.

Adolescents are often given jobs—such as emptying

wastebaskets or doing dishes—that provide them very little satisfaction of achievement. Their parents wonder why they mope, complain, and need to be chided to co-operate. Intent upon their own convenience and the necessity of getting things done, parents may fail to sense their children's maturing abilities and leave them out of the household planning—assigning them tasks as one would suggest to a little child that he wash his hands. Adolescents often call this "parent trouble," and it extends to parents' telling their children what to wear and what time to come in and how much to spend, and to nagging about anything from getting up in the morning to getting to bed on time at night. It is no wonder teen-agers give way to self-pity.

Youth leaders and adults can find ways to alleviate self-pity. . . . When youth leaders sense that there are adolescents in their group who are giving way to self-pity, they may sometimes lead to a discussion of the problem, by merely a comment, such as: "I heard some teen-agers on the bus talking about parent trouble, and I wondered what they meant." Perhaps, the group may decide to spend several sessions airing their difficulties and trying to see their parents' viewpoint. Some groups have invited their parents in for a clearinghouse session. This must be planned carefully so that a bit of humor can pervade the scene. Both parents and teen-agers need a fair chance to present their sides of issues over which there is trouble. Often just getting matters out into the open, in a situation not charged with the personal feelings of a particular moment, goes a long way toward relaxing the tension between the two ages and clearing the air for parents and their children to find positive solutions to their disagreements.

Another approach to the problem may be role playing—a device for freely putting oneself into a situation and working toward a solution. The leader outlines the situations which may be something such as this: Mrs. Thomas has gotten into the habit of nagging her daughter Phyllis each morning about getting up. She gave Phyllis an alarm clock for her birthday, and the agreement was that Phyllis would be responsible for getting to school on time. Mrs. Thomas thinks Phyllis should make her bed and tidy her room before leaving the house. She also wants Phyllis to eat an egg and toast, instead of only drinking a glass of juice and eating a cooky on the run. Phyllis sets the alarm clock for the latest possible moment and often doesn't have time for her room or breakfast. As soon as her mother hears she is up, she calls up the steps, "Better hurry! Your egg is ready. Don't forget to close the window in your room— and shut the bathroom door, so it will be warm when I want to bathe the baby."

Phyllis has been attending weekly sessions of the junior high guidance class where they've been studying how to get along with parents. She decides to quit pitying herself and do something about her troubles. She sets her alarm a little earlier than usual and gets up when it goes off. But that first morning she discovers the blouse she wants to wear is still damp from washing and is hanging in the basement. She goes scurrying to the basement calling to her mother to plug in the iron. When she returns, her mother begins her usual nagging.

At this point someone takes the mother's part and someone Phyllis's. The leader lets them continue in their roles until they have reached a successful conclusion or begin repeating themselves. The group then discusses how each acted, how they could have behaved differently and possibilities for different endings.

Role playing helps adolescents get to the root of their troubles by helping them face the facts of others' problems, so like their own. Then the truth about their behavior, and ideas for an objective solution can come to them; for then, defenses of their feelings are down.

Another aid to solving the problem of self-pity is to get teen-agers to put the facts on paper. In this way they can check those matters they would be capable of changing and can be challenged to watch for changes that occur in their parents' attitudes and actions.

Discussing the problems that self-pity raises in their development and in their relations with others may help adolescents want to solve their problems, rather than revert to martyr feelings.

Sometimes, simply having a sympathetic adult listener, and constructive guidance, will help a teen-ager see circumstances in their true light. After listening, a counselor may ask questions that make the teen-ager think about his responsibility in the matter, and he may be able to lead him to a decision to try for a solution. The teen-ager does not need pity—but the right kind of understanding attention to his feelings.

Worries and Fears

Worries and fears are responsible for some of the teen-ager's problems as he matures emotionally. He has learned pretty well to hide these real fears. They are not the ones he voices at home or in a group. They are the ones pushed from his conscious mind, or that he is ashamed of; and youth leaders and parents find them hard to discover. They hear about fears of not passing the tryouts, of not making the team, of failing a test or a course. These fears are socially acceptable, and a youth may voice them casually and without fear of betraying how he truly feels. But real fears, real anxieties, he may hardly admit even to himself—although they plague his consciousness when he least expects.

Sometimes the fear is that people don't really like him—or that he'll always be on the outside of the crowd looking in. His fear may be of an indefinable something which frightens and petrifies him just when he most wants to be socially at ease. He may fear being drafted or the imminence of war. Fanciful fears from childhood may still trouble him. Fear that his mother will die or that his home will be destroyed when he is away, or that his parents will quarrel, argue, and haggle over something he'd like to do—any of such fears may be the real problem.

For many teen-agers, fear is connected with their sexual development. Lack of proper sex instruction, as well as inadequate experiences of being loved, may trigger sex fears. An adolescent may fear he will lose his mind because he enjoys touching his body. He may fear that his parents and friends will find out, or that he will become ill or sterile. His guilt may go back to the time his mother slapped or tied his hands, when as a child he discovered the sensitiveness of his genitals. Or he may have received a verbal rebuff from his father. Now in adolescence, when most teen-agers—both boys and girls—rediscover the sensitiveness of their bodies, and the release of bottled-up feelings, fear may rise to plague him.

What can adults do to establish self-confidence and to help the adolescent overcome fears? In the problems of sex, youth need an understanding friend, one who appreciates their struggle. What all adolescents need is not freedom from impulses, but a balance of impulses, controlled and directed into worthy and right channels.

Consequently, to frighten young people, by suggesting that masturbation is a transgression, intensifies their guilt feelings, and limits their chances for breaking the pattern of anxiety and release. One of the most effective means of helping youth in this problem is to provide or suggest books which explain sexual development, and which include a sound approach to the problem of masturbation. Recent books, suitable for this age, with clear and simple discussions are listed at the end of the book.

SOCIAL GROWTH

This age group often finds itself out of gear with childhood friends, because of their maturing size. Furthermore, adults have not yet accepted them. Even though they may be physically quite mature, and though they have adult aspirations, they tend over and over again to make childish responses.

Dislike for the opposite sex persists through much of the early adolescent period, although girls' desire to be attractive to boys is gradually developing. There is a strong desire to be at ease in small social groups among both boys and girls. And within their own social group, strong feelings of self-sacrifice and loyalty arise.

Boys try to excel each other in physical skill, strength, bravery, and aggressiveness; and toward the close of the period they become conscious of social graces and personal grooming.

Thirteens desire solitude as well as social contacts. This is not because they want to limit their experiences with others, but because each experience must be relived within the privacy of their own thoughts.

They are only getting started in boy-girl relationships, and doing this is just like initiating other experiences. Adolescents are new to themselves, and it takes time and repetition and understanding to make the experiences satisfactory. Nancy said, "I'm slightly afraid of boys, and I can't seem to break through the solid wall that's there in the way." Carol said, "It's easier to talk with boys when you're doing something together, like working on a history project." Jim said, "I find it hard to be sociable when girls are around." And Dick complained, "I'm bashful and tense among girls. I can't talk."

Social poise and ease follow self-confidence, self-direction, and self-control. All of these, the adolescent is striving for, and will not attain until some years have elapsed. Often, the discovery that other girls and boys have similar problems, and boy-girl troubles, make a teen-ager feel less self-conscious. Experiences with the opposite sex, in groups of an informal nature, allow the teen-ager to gain poise and the ability to direct himself.

Youth leaders, who help these adolescents plan hikes, cook-outs, picnics, parties, tours, youth missionary projects, and Christian service activities, provide opportunities for them to make friends while doing something together. Church camps, community church choruses, junior high fellowships, and departmental parties and meetings can provide a natural environment for boys and girls to learn to work, worship, and play together in an easy manner. And the problem of topics for conversation solves itself.

When girls and boys observe each other as they officiate and co-operate in many and varied roles through church junior high activities, they begin to evaluate and choose the qualities and abilities they appreciate and would like to develop. Any activities that afford them opportunity to appraise and be appraised by the opposite sex are an important contribution to the early teen-ager. This evaluating is an important function of the thirteens' inwardizing, and forms the basis for effective self-appraisal and genuine thinking. They begin to make provisional decisions in the realm of moral conduct, deciding what is right and wrong, and their musings go on to include ideas, ideals, ambitions, and choices.

Thus they clarify and organize their social experiences and find themselves not so much at the mercy of their emotions as they once were. They sense their power to will and their growing ability to criticize their own performances. They are helped in bringing their thoughts to bear on their changing moods, their feelings and fears, and to maintain a neutrality about the opposite sex, although they are growing more critical and discriminating in the choice of friends in general.

Incessant talk—everywhere, anywhere—is the noticeable social development of teen-agers as they move into year fourteen. They exploit the intricacies of human personality, analyzing each other's traits, confessing, disputing, denying, talking about everybody. Though they may date only occasionally, and mostly in gangs, girls are talking about marriage and the personality traits of their husbands-to-be! They are anxious to be popular with their age-mates, and their devotion to the gang becomes a passion—especially if their drive toward emancipation from home controls becomes excessive. Fourteens travel in groups, even though the group may be in conflict with home, school, church, or community. Their identity with the group demands more loyalty than their identification with their homes. This in turn is counterbalanced by their insistent interest in their own development, which makes fourteens receptive to light thrown on their individual characteristics. They are conscious of the push of the growth forces at work within them. And as their powers of reasoning and the ability to think for themselves develop, they grow in ability to weigh the pros and cons of a problem—even their own—and come to a decision. They are sympathetic of the unpopular and unfortunate, and perceptive of human values and social obligations.

SHIFTING AFFECTION

Shifting affection from his parents to the group is an important process in these early adolescent years. This is not easy, and the adolescent makes many blunders and failures in his relations within his home and his group. It is not wise, therefore, to judge an adolescent by what he does, for the underlying cause of his action is often not too evident. When parents are oversolicitous in their love, or if they are negligent, or if one parent has died, an early adolescent may develop a crush on an adult, in lieu of wholesome friendships with his peers. Often the person on whom affection is bestowed is older and has the qualities the youth feels a parent should have. The youth may try to demand the constant attention of his adult friend and become quickly jealous when attention is shown to anyone else. Sometimes girls of the same age develop crushes on each other.

If affection that should begin to reach out to friends is thwarted and turned back on the parent, the adolescent may become dependent and immature. When he finally breaks away from his intense parental protection, he may seek someone on whom to transfer his fixed affection. If not outgrown in adolescence, this perversion may make the young person go through life seeking persons to cater to his emotional needs. A young person who has not experienced love in his home, or has experienced a possessive love, is often the victim of such crushes.

Here again leaders of young people can be helpful. If the crush is on the counselor, he should seek the company of others as soon as the young person comes on the scene. It is not helping the youth for the older person to return the emotion in kind. He needs a mature interest which will help him build independence for the future, and often this is best provided by including him in some group project which the youth leader supervises or directs, but where he is not an active participant. It is not always so simple, however, if the dependent feeling is deeply rooted. Then professional help from a guidance clinic or public school counselor should be sought.

It is dangerous to spurn the approaches of dependent adolescents, for it disorganizes their personalities. To give them no attention or affection, when they have had either none or too much, is not helping them. It is better to plan some constructive way to lead them out of themselves.

Often a counselor of youth may mistakenly interpret the admiration of a young person as being a crush. Because of the physical differences between boys and girls of this age, many girls have to direct their romantic yearnings toward boys they never see socially, or toward any male figure who seems personable to them—whether their high school teacher, the young farm hand on the next farm, the boy home from college for the summer, or a voluntary service worker. Often the object of such romantic devotion remains happily unaware of the love-dreaming; but when he does not, both he and the teenager will be happier if he can act as though he never guessed.

Though this may often seem amusing to adults, it is not a laughing matter to those going through it. It satisfies a perfectly healthy need in the girl at a time when she is not ready for the relationships involved in lasting love.

Boys go through this, too—only often a little later—and although not quite so whole-souled in their preoccupation, their talk is as much of girls as of sports.

The romance and falling in love imaginings of early teen-agers is not necessarily strongly associated with desire for physical expression. And as they grow older, just being together and talking is fascinating and satisfactory in the process of finding out what the other sex is like.

INTELLECTUAL GROWTH

The early adolescent's interests are broad. Twelves show increased ability over elevens in the use of ideas and concepts. The mechanics of math begin to intrigue them, and they will attempt definitions of abstract words. Their curiosity is immeasurable, and their learning is spurred by a natural urge to exercise their intellects. Coupled with their enthusiasm, which many consider the dominant trait of this earliest adolescent year, this bent to discover facts makes them ready learners.

Interest in reading climbs to a high peak by the thirteenth or fourteenth year; but the youth may then experience a new low because of his increased interest in movies, TV, and dancing, or because of his involvement in group activities within the church and elsewhere. As these adolescents become conscious of the great unknown they have not yet explored, they want to gorge their intellects with knowledge acquired by observation and experience. New concepts open suddenly—like grand vistas, leaving them breathless in the midst of an expanding world—and may seem to subside almost as quickly when another new interest captures their attention.

But another factor makes thirteens seem to change interest frequently. It is their need for mulling over, in the privacy of their own rooms, the experiences of their expanding lives.

Thirteens respond with intense interest to class discussions and assignments, and they acquire knowledge readily; but at home, and in odd moments, they are doing a lot of thinking things over. So many things are making their first impact upon them, they just cannot assimilate or register them automatically.

This inwardizing of thirteens leads to increased range of awareness. Fourteens will use words and phrases such as: in my opinion, it's my judgment, psychology says. They want their teachers to stress factual knowledge, but also to include panel discussions, which allow them to participate and express their ideas, opinions and study. They like class discussions which, more than answering the teacher's questions, involve themselves.

Their hunger for facts, their capacity for sustained attention, their ability to discuss, readiness to learn, and increased independence of thought make fourteens responsive pupils. Sunday-school and grade school teachers of eighth graders find them dynamic, challenging pupils.

Intellectual growth has significant implications for the parent, teacher, or leader. Within a group of junior-high students in a church or Sunday school a teacher-leader may have the enthusiastic twelve-year-olds, eager to discover facts; the inwardizing, perceptive thirteens, to whom the world seems too large to grasp; and the fourteen-year-olds who would like to discuss all the things they think and feel.

Individual differences within each age, which are bound to occur, add an additional educational problem. The early adolescents within one church group may come from a variety of junior highs, each with a different approach to education. Some pupils may be accustomed to group projects, others to strict recitation, and others to free discussion.

The wise teacher-leader seeks to help each child achieve within the scope of his abilities. He wants also to keep the more advanced abilities of older or quicker learners from stifling the interest of the others. He wants to meet the needs of each pupil. He must be quick to sense when differences in home religious training, previous Sunday-school attendance, or differences in public schools may make one child appear stupid and another seem to learn slowly. He will sense when age, difference in the color of skin, economic status, or ethnic origin may isolate a teen-ager from the group and hinder his learning. Any barrier that sets one child apart from the others of the group needs to be hurdled in one way or another for each child. Having a sense of belonging to the group is essential to his learning.

A teacher may discover one or two hands always raised in answer to his questions. Knowing that pupils should have the privilege of answering when they are prepared, he may find himself calling repeatedly on the same persons. Or, feeling that these pupils need less help, he may direct the question to another child, perhaps putting him on the spot. Such a situation demands that the teacher change from a technique of quizzing to one of discussion and group co-operation. Learning takes place in an atmosphere that allows each member to work within his capacities.

He may discover that asking the group to work together in two's, to discover the answers to a series of questions on a Scripture passage, will allow him freedom to assist those who need it and permit a slow learner to work with a faster one.

He may experiment with discussion, encouraging each member to participate when he has something to contribute—if only to share some past misconception or to voice a fear or to quote a Scripture verse or to tell how he feels about something. This is a relaxing way for learning to take place, and as each member feels more and more a part of the group, his participation will take on meaning both for him and the group.

Using the time allotted for Sunday school in ways as creative as the lesson material permits, will open up all sorts of off-the-beaten-track procedures for the teacher with problem learners.

And the results may be other than the usual dropouts, irregular attendance, and halfhearted interest apparent in the ordinary Sunday-school junior high department.

Perhaps the subject at hand would lend itself to working on projects—relief map of Palestine, diagrams of the temple or Jerusalem, drawings or descriptions of some portion of Jesus' life, time charts, scrapbooks of pictures of Palestinian life, keeping a notebook of discoveries in being a Christian. As each person volunteers to do a part of the project, he is using the skills that seem most natural to him and co-operating toward the completion of the project—not pitting his intelligence against that of his peers.

This kind of teaching requires advance preparation and planning on the part of the teacher. He must know the subject matter of a whole quarter of materials—not just the lesson for which he is currently preparing. He must be able to locate resource materials, supply files of pictures, know where facts can be found in the Bible, and make a lesson plan in advance of the class period. He must consciously criticize his methods, asking himself again and again, "Am I discovering and utilizing the unique contribution each child can make to this group? Am I helping him grow by stimulating his interest, using methods that take into account his abilities and status within the group? Am I accepting the feelings of each member and recognizing that as he feels, so to him things are?"

SPIRITUAL AWAKENING

The early adolescents' rapid growth, changing moods, and fact-gathering minds often constitute a problem for Sunday-school teachers. Sometimes they seem restless and unconcerned. Sometimes they ask questions for which the teacher feels they should already have the answers. They may seem disinterested.

Usually, beneath this surface minds are at work, turning over and over the spiritual truths youth has learned through example and teaching. Questions about religion may be troubling them. And they want a satisfactory philosophy of life. If they have already answered these, they may be pondering questions about community and world responsibility, about government and war and their relation to them.

In adolescence the spiritual cravings of the soul are strong. Frequently conflict exists between the adolescents' desire to do and their power to perform. Their knowledge of right and wrong has increased along with their emotional urges, and they awaken to a tremendous inadequacy in self. Petty stealing, lying, and dishonesty such as cheating are prevalent. Many adolescents find they are divided against themselves. They know what is right, but do not have the power to do it. They are gradually awakening to their spiritual need. And the climax comes when they become aware that they have broken the laws of God, and that their lives are displeasing to God.

Some adolescents react to conviction with violent opposition and postpone surrender. Others, with courage adults could hardly muster, admit conviction, and surrender their wills. Others seem to respond to nurture in an even, quiet manner, so that no problems seem to be evident. When God calls, they answer. This latter group may experience conflict and doubt later.

Thousands of boys and girls answer the call of the Spirit in this period and come to terms with the problem of sin and inner attitudes. In fact, the vast majority of conversions occur among persons in the adolescent period of life—the larger number by far, between the ages of ten and fourteen.

Prayers of godly parents, spiritual concern of youth leaders and Sunday-school teachers, and the sympathetic, understanding contacts of pastors all contribute to bringing adolescents to a conversion experience. And many are brought to a final decision for Christ by a chum. Young people are frequently the best soul-winners of other youth. And because of the interaction of the peer group, a young person may desire to join the church because his friends are joining, even though he may not yet have a conviction of sin.

In some church communities, joining church seems to be the proper social thing to do at a given age. This tradition itself raises problems in the life of the adolescent. He may be under conviction for several years before he reaches that age, then grow cold and indifferent by the time he arrives at the age considered proper to make his conviction known. Others may be members of a group who have become Christians, and, fearing they will be left without friends, they join with the majority.

Sometimes young people come into the church because they fear the doom of the unsaved, but do not sense Christ's love for them. Some, during an evangelistic campaign, may respond when pressed hard by a well-meaning Christian worker, but they do not necessarily have a call to repentance.

In congregations where discipline is rigid, junior-intermediates may resist the call of Christ in order to continue to participate in public school activities which the church forbids. Or they may postpone becoming Christians because church regulations will make them stand out as peculiar. This problem has been partly solved by the creation of schools for junior and senior high students within the church community. Where this is not the case, and Christianity's pattern is strict, the young person's conflict between the society of his church and the society of his school is heightened. There are always those who transfer their church loyalty, and those who drop out, without affiliating with another church group.

Boys and girls this age may leave the Sunday school and church for other reasons. Neglect at home, the influence of their peer group, becoming involved in social activities and entertainment outside the church group are but a few.

Other reasons may lie with the Sunday school and church. If their program does not meet the emotional, intellectual, spiritual, and social needs of these early adolescents, they will go or want to go somewhere else.

Each individual desires a foothold in someone's affections. If he cannot attain this in his home or Sunday school or church, he seeks it on the street, in his school, or in a club or gang. This is as true of girls as boys.

Herein lies a challenge for those who would claim adolescents for Christ. The Sunday school and church can offer opportunities for the early adolescent to make his group in the church an important contribution to the development of his life. The Sunday school and the church can adjust their program to the ways youth learn and expand their function to more than an hour's formal recitation over a Scripture passage.

Because his age group is so important to him, and

talking is so much a part of him, discussions become an effective means of learning and of social development. The Sunday-school curriculum is arranged to cover certain themes and Scripture passages. These may or may not happen to contain the answers to questions that are troubling a group at the particular time they are scheduled. And they have a function as content studies, that differs from the group-arranged discussion periods. But it remains imperative that intermediates have an opportunity for informal as well as formal learning. Some church organizations provide a weekly junior high fellowship, either on a week night or on Sunday evening. Where this has not been possible, some intermediate teachers have planned for weekly or biweekly class or department meetings. Here the teacher can become better acquainted with his group—allow them to organize in their own way, and plan meetings and discussions such as they feel they need.

In these groups, where the leader-teacher stands back and lets youth take the lead in planning, organizing, and directing, they feel more free to express their real interests. The leader's guidance and counsel can operate in quiet, unassuming ways when the group desires it. He is there as an aid to their orderly accomplishment of what they would like to do. He may help them find information on subjects they would like to learn more about, help them avoid dead-end streets, and to learn from their failures.

It is his task to perceive when they are struggling with a particular question and be ready with books, program suggestions, resource materials, and ideas of his own. He may be certain that the group will welcome this guidance—if they feel confident he will encourage them to work out the method and procedures for themselves.

When individuals feel a need to learn, then they are more likely to learn, psychologists tell us. Youth resist having their attention diverted from the interest that is most compelling at the moment. They want to discover the answers to their questions, and freedom to translate into action their feelings and ideas about the kind of persons they sincerely long to be.

Young people want to be fine people, liked by their friends and their families. They want to have confidence in themselves—to respect themselves. To have this, they must first receive it from their friends and families. When Sunday-school teacher-leader offers opportunities for early adolescents to bring their problems out into the open for discussion in an impersonal manner, he can help them mold the experiences and feelings of these formative years into the pattern of maturity they desire.

A youth leader can prepare the members of his group to recognize and answer the call of Christ when He speaks to them individually. He can help them gain the positive assurance that Christ will call each one individually, that He is ready to forgive their sins, to accept their repentance, and to offer them power to live pleasing to Him. A youth leader can thus prepare his group to listen for God's voice and to understand what God is asking them to do.

Because they do not have a balanced emotional expression in religious experience, true worship experiences need to be planned for early adolescents so that there is not an overemphasis of the emotional element. The most powerful emotions in man are raised in religious experience. Through these, God can lead youth into lives of great usefulness, if they have not been indiscriminately tampered with.

Campfire services where each individual is given a stick to put on the fire to show his readiness to become a flame for God, or variations of the same procedure, can embarrass intermediates to whom God has not yet spoken, or who do not understand what is really meant. Revival meetings that are prolonged unduly can destroy the innate beauty of a young person's hearing and answering God's voice.

Conversion is the fruit of definite Bible teaching and spiritual nurture, either in the home, the church, or the Sunday school. It is not high-pressuring salesmanship. The youth's experiences of yearning and aspiration, his guilt, unrest, and dissatisfaction with himself, his longing for understanding, and his need for reconciliation and for contact with a power greater than himself—these are God's natural means of preparing youth for a genuine acceptance of the Lord Jesus Christ. If youth has been taught that Christ offers acceptance, love, forgiveness, and peace, and that in His own life and teaching He answers many puzzling questions, youth will listen for God's voice and hasten to answer His call.

For the adolescent God is a person he could see, if he could see the other side of a wall or a mountain.

Before adolescence, the child lived mostly in the world of what he saw and felt physically. His feelings toward God were much the same as those he had toward his earthly parents and those adults in positions similar to that of his father. If his earthly father's love was consistent when the child obeyed or disobeyed, if his forgiveness was quick and genuine and waiting for the child to accept, and if his discipline was understandable and protective, then as the child becomes an adolescent, he is in a good position to understand God's laws of love and forgiveness. His thankfulness can embrace God's mercy and love—His kindness and everlasting forgiveness to those who come in true repentance for their selfishness and wrongdoing.

To these teen-agers, God is very near. And in the warmth of their new experience of answering God's call they have faith and confidence in all God's promises. The spiritual relationship and the mystical union of man with his Maker come much later in the normal development of the adolescent.

Growing in Worship

These early adolescents, newly come to faith in Christ, need help with private devotions to keep alive the spark of devotion that conversion has kindled. Their lives are busy with activities they plan and with those their schools and homes plan for them. They may ambitiously aim to spend their future in God's service, but allow their present to be feverishly burned up in activities.

Some complain, "The Bible is so dry I can't get anything out of it." Others say, "My mind wanders when I

read, and I never know where to find something to help
me." Some prefer devotional books to the Bible. Some
need a method for reading and studying that is more
meaningful than simply trying to struggle through the
books of the Bible in order. Others can't seem to fit
Bible reading and meditation and prayer into the daily
program.

These problems are familiar to every young Christian
and to many older ones as well. Many Christians neglect
the Bible because they do not understand it or do not
know how to get help from it. The King James Version,
so familiar in our homes, employs many expressions that
are not familiar to our present generation of young
people. The home library as well as the Sunday-school
library should include translations in language that is
more easily understood. Youth should be encouraged
to read from more than one translation. A helpful
group activity would be to have the same Scripture portion read by various persons, each reading from a different translation. Individuals might be encouraged to
buy different translations in order to carry this out successfully. The use of different translations is often a
means of increasing understanding and appreciation of
the Word.

A youth leader, who senses that his group is having
difficulty, can raise the question, perhaps in a way such
as this: He may hear the group talking about the hour
their parents are asking them to come in at night—and
how they want to push the hour later for parties. When
he makes an assignment after a Sunday-school session,
and someone groans, he can ask, "When will you do

4

this—when you have your private devotions?" The group will probably look blank—but perk up when he continues, "I don't see how you ever find time for devotions—with all you have to do."

Here is understanding—not criticism and condemnation. Someone from the group may say, "We don't; I haven't read my Bible for weeks." The leader can put more sympathetic understanding into another question, "Are the rest of you in the same predicament?" When they nod in agreement, he can suggest that perhaps they'd like to discuss the matter at their next weekly meeting and maybe they can help each other.

At this meeting he should have ready a check list of common private devotion problems. They can decide which they want to discuss and in what order. Perhaps this session can expand to include discussions on how to read with a purpose, how to find a method of Bible study that each can enjoy, an introduction to different methods of Bible study, and experimentation with different versions of the Bible, comparing them with the King James.

Questions about prayer are sure to arise, and the leader can make note of these for later discussion. They will likely include, Why doesn't God answer my prayers? Why should we pray "for Jesus' sake"? How do I know God is listening and will answer? Why can't I keep my mind from wandering when I pray?

Books and source materials to guide your group should include a Bible dictionary, Bible atlas, a harmony of the Gospels, *Profitable Bible Study* by Wilbur Smith, *How to Enjoy Studying the Bible* by Joseph M. Gettys,

Greatest Story Ever Told by Fulton Oursler, and *Youth Program Ideas,* volumes *1, 2, 3, 4,* issued by Herald Press. Volume 2 includes plans for four sessions on private devotions. The plans include directions for using a Bible dictionary, atlas, commentary, and concordance; ideas for sharing devotional helps; and a worship project. Although these plans are geared for formal sessions, they can be useful in providing ideas and the basis for informal discussions of younger teens.

Another problem that hinders teen-agers' private worship is that of grappling with personal temptations. A leader may realize, from the discussion on prayer and Bible reading, that his group is troubled about overcoming temptations. Perhaps a member will say, "I get so mad at my brother, I don't want to read my Bible," or, "When I'm thinking about something I want to do, I don't find time for devotions." Youth in this age group are tempted to cheat, to gossip, to get mad, to drive before they are legally permitted to do so, to be mean to their brothers and sisters, to talk back—to argue. They spend a lot of time arguing with themselves and among themselves—wondering why they can't do this or that, and all the time, feel inwardly prompted not to, but nevertheless try to find sanction from parents, or the church or school or friends, to make it right for them.

The book, *Teens! How to Meet Your Problems* (listed at the end of the book), suggests answers for particular problems ranging from troubles inside the family, through troubles with friends, at school, and deep within oneself, to feeling different, moody, angry, discouraged, friendless, rejected, and ill. The first program idea in *Youth Program Ideas,* Volume *1* is entitled "This Year for Christ" and deals with the temptation to let Christianity become second to other things. *Right or Wrong* is a book that gives pros and cons on all sorts of problem-making recreational activities, such as commercial sports, movies, and dancing.

Money, with which many teen-agers are flush, presents all sorts of temptations both for those who have it and for those who don't. The youth leader may be confronted with serious complications because of differences in spending abilities among members of a group. Sometimes the situation can be eased only by informal and casual discussion of how God wants Christians to think about money.

Milo Kauffman's book, *The Challenge of Christian Stewardship,* has a wealth of illustrations and arguments for disciplined giving. *Youth Program Ideas, 2,* contains ideas and plans for several discussions on this theme. They are entitled, "Dollars and Sense." Facts about current teen-age spending habits have been published in numerous magazine articles. A quick look in an index to periodicals in a public library should locate an article to bring the facts about their spending to the attention of a youth group.

Early teens can be led to add to their worship experience the joy of consistent, dedicated giving. Participation in the weekly dedication of gifts and offerings to the Lord, during the Sunday morning worship, will be more meaningful for those who have carefully laid aside a portion for the Lord.

As early teen-agers' earning and spending powers increase, they need to recognize these abilities as gifts from God and dedicate them to Him. Consistent record-keeping of their earnings, spending, and giving can be made a part of their daily private worship. A youth leader, who helps early teen-agers develop the habit of committing to God each new area of life as it unfolds, is laying the basis for them to have fruitful private and public worship experiences all through life.

Books for Early Teen-agers

A leader can make a significant contribution to teen-agers who are hesitant to voice their problems in a group by starting a small library shelf with a simple file box for the book cards. Here the teen-agers can pick a book to browse through or take with them. Sources for such books could be the church library, the counselor's library, or the library of a pastor or other interested adult.

The number of books should not be large—but the books need to be up-to-date. For keeping track of books, a card in the pocket of the book, to be signed with the borrower's name and placed in the file box under the author's name will prove sufficient and simple. Teen-agers like the privacy and simplicity of serving themselves, and a book that receives acceptance will make the rounds without the teacher having pushed it. Books that do not move should be removed, perhaps to be re-inserted on the shelf at a later time. A list for this shelf should include those listed at the conclusion of this book.

Chapter 3

Middle Adolescence
Years 15 to 17

As YOUTH enter middle adolescence individual differences become more pronounced. The slow pupil reaches his intellectual level, so that school may be difficult for him. The brilliant scholar may be ready for college by the time he is halfway through middle adolescence.

Hereditary characteristics of face and form introduce the appearance of the adult. Emotionally, some may be eleven or twelve-year-olds, while physique presents an adult. Others, more precocious socially, may marry before the close of the period. Some gain economic independence and become job seekers, while others remain dependent even into the latter part of later adolescence. Many characteristics that are true of early adolescence may still be found in youth of these ages—fifteen to seventeen—and many develop amazingly toward the maturity of later adolescence.

Youth, passing off the scene of early adolescence, seek

to achieve unity of personality. They realize the need for increased co-ordination in desire and impulse, and for unity of purpose. "Sometimes I think," said Irene, "I'd like to be a dietitian, but I like nursing and teaching, too. There are so many things I'd like to be," she concluded with a sigh. It is not uncommon to find even at the close of this period, that the adolescent has made little progress toward a unity of purpose, although he has thought deeply and experimented much. He is faced with the task of making some of the major adjustments in life. Sociologists find these needed adjustments to be quite universal among all peoples:

1. Achieving freedom from home and family.
2. Choosing friends among both sexes.
3. Directing activity into useful channels.
4. Establishing unity of thought and life.
5. Entering into a vital religious experience.

Thrust out into this great sea of decisions, it is surprising that boys and girls ever reach maturity well-balanced, noble, and pure. Any of these adjustment areas may disturb youth. Any one of them may spell catastrophe if they are not resolved. Therefore, Christian parents, teachers and youth leaders find in these years a matchless opportunity.

PHYSICAL CHANGE

In early adolescence we observed the uneven tides of emotional and physical energy. Girls reach their zenith of growth in height; but boys, even though they begin their rapid growth in the middle of early adolescence, do not keep pace with the girls.

Thus, by middle adolescence, the girls find themselves in possession of a rather even flow of energy. This may, or may not, be true emotionally. Boys continue to grow rapidly, well into their fifteenth year. Additional small gains continue until eighteen or later. Gains in weight are realized well on into later adolescence. For the girls, growth is almost complete at sixteen in both height and weight.

On their fourteenth birthday, 90 per cent of the girls are sexually mature. At the same age, only 50 per cent of the boys have passed this stage. And not until sixteen have boys gained the percentage of 90. The difference in body growth of adolescents presents a variation in emotional, social, and economic maturity between the sexes of the same age, and explains the air of superiority girls carry toward boys their age.

The lungs and heart keep pace with the general rapid growth, enabling them to increase the supply of oxygen and energy. The stomach, too, keeps apace of the generous appetite, which does not abate much before the eighteenth year. Stomach discomforts and odd ideas about food are common to this age. A girl may decide that she cannot digest fish; a boy may turn away from tomato soup and even the stand-by peanut butter. Occasionally, this is due to some deficiency, but usually it is caused by overeating or improper diet. The soda fountain takes the adolescent's time and appetite, but hardly provides an adequate diet.

Vitality in this period is very high, although not so high as in early adolescence. However, the death rate is influenced some by accidents occasioned by the new freedom of the middle teens. Firearms, automobiles, swimming pools, industry—all these claim many lives yearly from this group.

By later adolescence the average youth has matured physically. The boy has acquired the rich voice of masculinity. His hair is more glossy, and there is a glint in his eye that did not exist before. Shaving has become routine. His shoulders are broad and the boyish lines are gone. His hands and feet no longer cause him embarrassment. He has become big brother to his admiring little brother and sister. The girl, too, is entirely at home with herself, physically. She strives to be graceful and self-composed—and beautiful.

EMOTIONAL PROGRESS

Chronological age marks the milestones of maturity. To adolescents, one year makes a great deal of difference. Each birthday means more freedom, less restraint. If a middle teen-ager is asked his age, he will invariably reply, "I will be so and so on my next birthday." The Sunday-school superintendent knows the easy offense that is given when young people of this age are not properly graded—where age is the standard.

To make emotional maturity the standard of progress does not occur to adolescents, probably because standards of emotional maturity for each age group are not clearly discernible. Young people may label their own friends as square, even though they do not expect emotional maturity of each other. They have their own ways of judging, of accepting or rejecting.

Before youth can attain social independence, he must

achieve it emotionally. Some of his problems of this period have been gaining proportion throughout childhood. Making decisions and abiding by them cheerfully whatever the consequences is still often difficult. If he is growing, the adolescent is making decisions without consulting everyone, especially when the matter is small. Adolescents who still would like their decisions readymade and handed to them have not advanced toward emotional independence.

If he is growing, the middle adolescent is also able to adjust to new situations with relative ease. In fact he often seeks new situations, seceding from the family circle, skimping greetings, keeping to himself, resisting restraints and restrictions however reasonable, engaging parents in a cold war of varying degrees of intensity, and venting his belligerence by dashing out—out to the gang and whatever they can find to do.

Fifteens feel that they are growing up. They do not want to be considered children. They want freedom— especially tonight and tomorrow night. And, whether they get it or not, in their imaginative minds they will often attend a school in a distant town.

Their emotions about home are all mixed up. They want to outgrow dependence on home, yet they feel the old emotional attachments.. And as they grow toward the social groups outside home, their behavior at home may reach an all-time low. Yet they feel anguish when parents disagree or don't get along, for they are identifying themselves with the adult roles of parents and developing ideas of marriage and career.

The middle adolescent is extremely sensitive to his

environment. He is awaking from the idealistic dreams of early adolescence and discovering that the world is full of stark realities. His growing sense of self-dependence seems to underline his dependence on others, and the resulting problem is to resolve the difficulties as well as he can on his own resources.

Sixteens and seventeens usually have discovered their own particular gifts and interests. They have found ways of achieving self-respect, either through school or other pursuits, so that their emotional independence is recognized by parents. They achieve a higher status because they are more self-reliant and self-assured. Their spirit of independence matures to a satisfying sense of interdependence. Although they still prefer the company of their friends to that of their families, the dissatisfied, uncertain, rebellious attitude is gone: and parents are usually more willing to go their way and let these sixteens and seventeens go theirs.

By the end of this middle adolescent period, youth have their emotions pretty well under control. They are not given to worries; their moods are light and fleeting; they seldom cry. Anger is curbed by walking away or laughing it off. They enjoy laughter and social situations, and they are friendly, cheerful, and outgoing.

They are sensitive to other people, and thus others tend to get along with them. They are beginning to sense and appreciate the motives of their friends and parents. They will make allowances for others, yet recognize the importance of both written and unwritten codes of conduct.

FEELINGS OF INSECURITY

Feelings of insecurity and inferiority may result if a middle adolescent is halted and confused in this process of gaining emotional independence. The causes of insecurity are many and usually deep and hidden from view. Sometimes the early reason has disappeared, but the effect remains.

The roots of insecurity may reach back to an unnamed fear in childhood—caused by the state of mind of the parents. When parents fear they cannot supply material needs, they may impart to their children an uneasiness about food, clothes, and shelter, that reaches into other areas of the teen-ager's life.

Differences of opinion between parents concerning discipline, and unpredictable parental punishment, robs youth of stability. If one parent punishes and the other interferes, or if the parents severely punish at one time and then at another laugh at the same offense, or if the child is punished and then indulged, he never knows what to expect.

"I never know what is right," said Mary. "Father can see my point of view—at least he tries to—but Mother always criticizes everything and scolds me when I do what she feels is wrong. Sometimes I think she is just jealous of Father's love for me."

Doubt as to the honesty of adults brings insecurity. Children must be able to respect their parents. If they feel they cannot trust them, their foundations are weakened or removed. Sara suffered repeated failure in her Christian life, because, it turned out, her father lived a good life to the public and to his church; but his sins were open to the eyes of his family who was to act as though he were perfect.

Science teachers sometimes undermine youth's faith. They present many theories; and, in the name of science, they leave the decision to the student. Because adolescents are limited in experience and immature in methods of arriving at truth, their faith may be uprooted in the process.

In the climate of domineering parents a child may become insecure. The more aggressive children may leave because they cannot tolerate suppression. Then the more co-operative ones, who should have the opportunity to develop independence, get the full force of the domination. It is surprising, sometimes, that such young people, when taken out from under this parental management and control, are able to achieve emotional independence.

Wrong attitudes about sex can create insecurity. It is a tragedy that many parents—with studied care—refuse to share the real facts concerning the origin of life, and even misinform their children. It is no wonder that the miscellaneous information adolescents have gathered often makes them fearful of their sex feelings and distrustful of their reactions. Gilbert Youth Research, in 1957, reported that 76 per cent of teens never discuss the facts of life with their parents, yet youth admit that often the number one problem between boys and their girl friends is the sex problem.

Feelings of inferiority may also result from poor emotional adjustments. Family financial failures, poverty, and low social status or environment, or parents who do not get along, may make a youth feel inferior to his peers. An incident that brings disgrace to a family can damage an adolescent's security. More subtle, and deeper than all these, may be the fact that parents and friends have refused to accept the youth and his aptitudes and abilities and limitations, so that he is afraid to accept himself. Human nature wants to be superior. When the adolescent senses he cannot achieve what his parents desire, he may retreat into himself, blame his family or heredity, and fail to utilize the abilities he has.

To help youth who are caught in these cross currents, youth leaders must know how feelings of insecurity can be recognized in a teen-ager's behavior. Insecure individuals have difficulty adjusting to new situations. They have difficulty making up their minds, and may decide and redecide a half dozen times before they act. Even then, they often may not be satisfied that they did the right thing. They will attempt to make others decide issues for them. They may fear to leave home.

On the other hand, insecure individuals may be extremely conservative, dogmatic, and intolerant, for they fear change. Their insecurity may express itself in lack of goals, in restlessness, and dissatisfaction with any work. Or it may make them emphasize little details and fritter away time and energy at little tasks in order to avoid facing real issues. A girl with a composition to write may give minute attention to trying on a new dress or cleaning out a dresser drawer, because she doesn't want to settle down to solid work. But if every assignment is evaded by other "necessary" activities, she is probably caught by the fear of not succeeding.

The insecure are often hero-worshipers and seem unable to see in their friends anything but rosy perfection, giving them a sort of dog devotion.

Young people who feel inferior are often self-conscious and bashful. They may studiously avoid contests, whether athletic or intellectual, refuse to accept responsibility and give many reasons other than the real ones. They may resort to ill health, plead they are too busy, or that they do not have proper clothes, when the real reason is a sense of social inadequacy.

Some middle adolescents openly and frankly express inferiority, embracing it as something that cannot be cured, avoided, or evaded. Some seek help from anyone who will take the time to go to the root of the trouble with them. Others pretend self-confidence, are critical of everything and everybody, and often carry chips on their shoulders, taking every comment as personal, meant to give them offense. These individuals may resort to teasing, bullying, boasting, or being aggressive to make impressions and compensate for their own feelings of inadequacy. Inferiority may make another youth begin things and never finish, because he fears the finished product will not meet approval. Out of these feelings spring jealousy, envy, lying, stealing, cheating, and the aggressive actions characteristic of delinquency. They are all used as means to cover up the real self.

In America, 10 per cent of the 16,000,000 teen-agers get into trouble with the police; for middle adolescence is a vulnerable period of development. Wildness seems to be in the adolescent's nature as he strives for emotional independence and maturity and fights his feelings of inadequacy and insecurity. If parental influence, his inner self, the values he has somehow gained as he grew up, and society's influence do not keep him from violence, he will fall into the hands of the law.

For these teen-agers and many others, there is only a dim line between having fun and delinquency. Teen-agers have become professionals at leisure. They have the money and the time—and the example of their parents. And they have more energy. With money jingling in their pockets, their father's car at their disposal, and plenty of places to go and things to see, what makes them become delinquent? Boredom, insecurity, and inner anxieties, that make teen-agers call attention to themselves, their fears, and their problems of growing up emotionally, all contribute to the problem.

Wild, outrageous conduct is a bold proclamation that the adolescent is at the end of his rope emotionally, that his fears have become unmanageable, that he is badly in need of help. Only a skilled and sympathetic specialist such as a school counselor, public health nurse, or child welfare worker can discover his frustrations; the family physician might help by referring parents or youth leaders to a source of psychiatric help to get at the roots of the insecurity.

But youth leaders can be of inestimable help to 90 per cent of the adolescents in the throes of growing up, whose insecurity is not so deeply rooted. The adolescents' self-criticism and evaluation of others make them experimental psychologists. They crave guidance, particularly guidance that doesn't come from the home circle. They want objective knowledge of human behavior and human nature and seem capable of sensing where it fits their needs without being told.

The middle adolescent's sensitivity to individual differences, his preoccupation with what his eventual career will be, and his new interest in extracurricular activities make him an extremely educable subject.

He will respond to studies in psychology which aid his understanding of the forces at work within him. There are numerous books available in this field. *My Dear Ego* (see bibliography) is written in a simple direct fashion, with bits of humor, to help the reader see that everyone is in part egocentric, and to form an image of his own personality. *Youth Program Ideas, 2* contains two programs on emotional maturity entitled "Know Yourself" and "Take Yourself in Hand," which include discussion questions, ideas for skits to introduce the problems, and quizzes to help youth rate themselves. Illustrations and correlated devotional plans are also included. *Face Your Life with Confidence* is a collection of counsels for youth; its fifty-one short chapters embrace problems of founding one's faith, getting along with oneself and family, fitting into the group and with the other sex, and reaching goals. Because the book is based on case histories, the discussions about problems can be kept objective.

As young people sense that everyone operates within limitations of ability, education, skills, and economics, they are more ready to accept their own limitations and try to overcome feelings of inferiority. They will sense that feelings of inadequacy may be closely connected

5

with their pride—their "dear egos," and perhaps they will be able, at times, to smile at the game they are playing with themselves—and be freed to be themselves.

Young people can find God a very present help in trouble. Youth leaders can help them to formulate prayers for times when fear, discouragement, anger, feelings of inferiority and insecurity, desperation, or wildness take hold of them.

As part of the devotional period following a discussion of growth problems, the leader can introduce the discipline of each person writing a prayer for a particular need he feels. Examples of prayers for particular situations can be found in inexpensive but valuable books such as *The Golden Book of Prayer,* and *Prayers, Ancient and Modern.*

An individual young person who seeks guidance should be welcomed by a youth counselor with sincerity and a listening ear. Friendly recognition outside youth meetings will establish confidence and rapport and enable the youth leader to learn about the interaction of the group and to see each individual's qualities of personality. It will invite the confidence of those who have particular problems they would like to talk over with the youth leader.

The young person who lingers after a meeting, the youth who offers some unasked assistance may be seeking a chance to chat privately with the youth leader. But he may have difficulty getting started talking about his problem. A question such as, "How is life treating you?" or "How are you getting along in your Christian life?" may relieve the tension.

The counselor can aid the interviewee to unload by asking him questions that prove his interest and mirror his feelings. The counselor reserves his opinion and never injects a similar experience he has had. His task is to help the counselee discover exactly what his problem is and to find a solution. Understanding sympathy and sensitive appreciation of the interviewee's predicament is the counselor's contribution to the counselee's discovery of how he can solve his problem.

Listening is an art every would-be counselor of youth must learn. Facial expression and the movement of the eyes portray to the counselee whether he is being heard with the ears or with the mind and heart. As the leader puts himself in the place of the youth and sees the problem from his point of view, his face will portray his empathy. His comments will assure the counselee that he is being understood. The counselor must not be shocked at anything that the counselee may say, nor by word or look contribute to the counselee's guilt, or condemn him. As he refrains from expressing his personal feelings and prejudices, and feels with the counselee, he will aid him to come to grips with his real problem. He must be alert to detect whether the real problem has been stated or whether a smaller one has been presented as a screen. Young people may never reveal their real problems if they feel misunderstood, criticized, or condemned in the minor problem they present first.

As the interviewee presents his troubles, the problem gradually begins to unfold to the leader. But it may take more than one interview for the young person to be able to diagnose and look at his problem objectively. The leader questions, helping the young person suggest possible solutions. He encourages the interviewee to step out on his own in putting the problem into words and in formulating a positive program of action.

The counselee should leave with new courage to proceed by himself. He should feel the assurance that he is welcome to return, not so much for the further solution of his problem, but perhaps to discuss his progress in following the plan of action he decided on and to discuss any other problem.

The leader can also, by observation, a casual question, or perhaps by a passing comment later, discover whether all is well, and whether the counselee is solving his problem.

The best advertisement for a leader's ability to interview is the person he has interviewed. The word is passed on to others—whether good or otherwise. Youth is quick to detect if a leader keeps confidence, if his interest is sincere. They readily accept one who makes an honest attempt to understand and aid them.

Social Growth

Middle teens chum around in groups. Where one is, there are all the rest. They dress and behave just like their peers. They use the same vocabulary. They spend their money for the same things. They have the same worries and the same aversions. They all think that there's nothing to do in the home town, yet they never have enough time to do all they want to do.

What these gangs think matters. It matters almost

more than what parents say, and in the end, it probably determines whether teen-agers even listen to their parents' endless haranguing. When they aren't with the gang, they are on the telephone. For friends give them that essential sense of belonging, and their basic entertainment is talk—about other teen-agers, about teachers, about heroes, the latest records or popular songs.

A big reason why teens want to appear just like their friends is that they are very sensitive to being different. Thereby they gain a sturdier sense of security, appearing more alike than different. And, in their struggle to find the meaning of the new impulses driving them toward maturity, they need the healthy fellowship of others like themselves. As someone has said, in this company of mutuals is the best soil for the roots of courage; and a valuable outgrowth is a firmer, healthier belief in themselves, mankind as a whole, and God. These three usually go together, and if one is missing or nearly lost the other two are low also.

The protecting walls of the group usually enclose those of equal social or economic standing. Here prestige and acceptance lend a certain distinction to each individual. This differs from the science, photography, art, or French club that just anyone can get into. It is a bulwark against the disapproval and criticism—or the mere passivity—that middle teens feel from adults. Here they do not feel lonely or defenseless. Here they feel the backing of friends.

The associates on the outside, especially of a church group, are the ones youth leaders must be alert to—for they are always precariously close to the line where the church holds no influence for them and they may drop out altogether. These teen-agers are rarely able or equipped to draw a circle that will take in the friends they so much desire would take them in. They may be ashamed, or financially unable, to invite the group to their homes. They may be financially unable to dress as the group, or to spend as the group, or to act with the same freedom when the group is making plans for camping trips, excursions, parties.

They may be on the outside because conditions other than money have put them into a different social strata. Living in the mountains instead of in the valley, being born of nonchurch or non-Christian parentage, being from a different race or of a different color, any of these may isolate a teen-ager.

His only help lies in finding some way to diminish the difference and increase his similarity, identity with, and acceptance by his peers, if this is possible.

Sometimes a church youth leader can operate in unobtrusive ways to help the youth without funds find employment. Sometimes, tipping off a conscientious member of the in-group to the ultimate significance of this person being left out makes a difference in the way he is treated.

A variation of this technique is used for getting a certain product, record, or even a personality started on a popularity spree. A manufacturer gets a popular girl on an important campus to wear a certain kind of sweater and influence her gang to wear the same—and it isn't long until the sweater is taking hold and the manufacturer is certain of a market.

Where a youth is shunned because his clothes are different, the introduction of uniform robes for choruses sometimes alleviates the distress of the group over what an individual may wear on certain occasions.

Sometimes a youth leader must work in obvious ways, perhaps asking to speak to the youth council and laying the problem before them. Often the sensitive understanding of the youth leader for the feelings on both sides of the problem will lead to sincere cooperation of the youth council in finding a solution.

There are times when a youth may feel on the outside, even though the group thinks of him as in. Then particularly can a youth council find ways to help this youth make some contribution that will bring him recognition and make him feel truly a part of the in-group.

Teen-agers want to be accepted and liked. They need friends with whom they can exchange ideas, share things, or go places. Friends help them find their place in life, and lead them to new techniques for understanding people—and thus to understanding themselves. Friends fill some of their most heartfelt needs, for sincere interest and concern for their friends broadens and deepens their own vision and experience.

Building friendships is not always easy—even for those who are within the sheltering walls of a group. Young people respond to formal and informal discussion of "How Can I Make Friends?" And the youth leader needs to be prepared to offer a variety of suggestions for making this a profitable study. If he keeps a file of articles clipped from magazines, church papers, and newspapers—and makes a note of the chapters and sections of books that deal with this subject and drops it in this file also, he will never be without up-to-date material. This is a current as well as an old subject, and writers are ever giving it new treatment. Program plans also will be found in *Youth Program Ideas* and in *Youth Fellowship Kits* (Programs and Topics, Westminster Press).

Other denominational program-planning materials will offer varied approaches to this and other areas of study, such as vocations, the church and community, world brotherhood, fellowship, outreach, stewardship, witnessing, personal spiritual growth, and faith.

DATING PATTERNS

Young people are greatly interested in love and the possibilities it holds for their future happiness. They are on the threshold of many social decisions. Although sometimes they seem not to sense that future happiness depends in part upon their present decisions, they are concerned for their future. It becomes the task of the Christian youth counselor to help youth follow God little by little, as they take what seems to them simple steps, so they will ultimately grow toward maturity and the one great social decision.

Dating of teen-agers took a sophisticated turn at our mid-century. According to some studies the high-school crowd today goes steady—an approximate 60 per cent of them. And although any one of the crowd may have three or four steadies during a year, while they are dating, they like the date insurance which going steady gives them.

Others go steady because it bolsters their morale and self-respect and proves their desirability. Some insist that it is economical and a lot less bother, and if teen-agers know how to behave, it is not dangerous. Besides, some girls complain that once a girl is seen with a boy several times, no other boy will date her, so why not go steady?

Parents and sociologists and other interested adults object that it limits a teen-ager's friends just when they think he should have a wide social experience. They fear that it promotes petting and that it is pretty silly for teen-agers, who have achieved little intellectual insight and emotional maturity, to act out the role of adults.

Some have pointed out possible benefits. Perhaps a carry-over of the intense monogamous feelings of these teen-agers may stabilize their future marriages. Others have discovered that these steady steadies are less serious than some adults may suppose them to be, even though the couple is openly affectionate. But those who think these affairs are only puppy love have failed to notice how seriously youth take them. When they are in love—or think they are—or wondering whether they are—they want adults to accept their feelings for what they are, even though they may never marry any of their high-school steadies.

Because the Christian teen-ager is just learning to govern his new emotions, he may blunder a great deal, tending to respond to individuals who give him the greatest immediate satisfaction, rather than be governed by eternal values. He may have intense temptations to experiment in sex. When his information is unscientific and has not been wholesomely imparted, and his imagination has free reign, he is likely to be pushed out of bounds by his fanciful dreaming. On the other hand, where adolescents know the facts of life and love, and have grown up in an atmosphere where love has been wholesomely expressed, their inner restraint and high ideals tend to negate their desire to experiment. When fellows and girls this age go out of bounds in petting and sex experimentation, it is usually because they feel insecure or are rebellious.

Association between the sexes often results in extreme infatuations. Couples seek each other's company constantly and think themselves very much in love. These couples are dating to date; to find out what the other sex is like; to experiment with mature relationships; to find out about themselves.

By far the greater number of friendships will not be lasting. Couples soon weary of each other; or economic, educational, and parental restrictions serve to postpone marriage and call a halt to the friendship. Others fall in love with love, read of romance, and enjoy the thrill of living it. Others may go steady, just to be dating—all the while secretly despising each other.

Social gatherings of the senior high school group are scenes of action and color. Boundless energy calls for activity, and without it entertainment is a failure. Within the fellowship of church groups teen-agers enjoy ping-pong, shuffleboard, tennis, skating, softball, basketball, and football—whether as spectators or participators.

Pastors and youth leaders who accept the dating

habits of youth can encourage their couples to engage in discussion groups after the Sunday evening services. Some have arranged for informal discussion of the pastor's sermon following the service. These groups meet in the basement of the church or parsonage and the young people take turns serving tea or coffee. Youth leaders can encourage couples to attend youth fellowship meetings together. Some youth leaders make a point of suggesting to their committees that informal meetings must include games and activities that couples can play together. They also take couples into account when hikes, picnics, camping trips, etc., are planned.

The church's responsibility to youth includes creating an environment in which young people can grow toward maturity through wholesome associations. When a social room can be made available in the church or in the home of the pastor or youth leader, or in a basement, no end of benefits can accrue to the young people themselves and to the church as a whole.

Depending on its location this room can be used for after-church activities, evening get-togethers, group meetings, crafts and hobbies, singing, quiet games, reading, or talking for couples and for anyone who wants to be with friends.

Getting the room into shape often stirs the enthusiasm of the group, brings offers of skills, time, furniture, money, and ideas, and welds the group into a working team.

Service projects—a Lord's acre, participation in a mission program, supervising younger children's groups within the church, visitation at convalescent, old people's, and children's homes, or community service—not only serve their particular purpose, but they also make possible association of couples, while providing an outlet for their energies.

Middle teen-agers, allowed the freedom of "buzz" groups, panel discussions, and situation drama, and the privacy of separate meetings for fellows and girls as the subject matter determines, are anxious to study sex, love, and marriage. Pamphlets that get at these subjects in a wholesome, friendly way, may serve as a basis for discussion and study sessions and a background for lectures and films (see bibliography).

Recreational Habits

Commercial entertainment, so available from the corner drug to the school stadium, has taken its toll in the spiritual growth of young Christians. Joe said, "When I was seventeen I purchased a car, and I enjoyed every amusement possible. I skated at the rink, bowled, and went to the pool and beach. I finally started movie attendance. This resulted in conflict with my conscience. Sometimes this led me to my knees in despair." Fortunately, Joe found the Lord again, but not until later adolescence, when he discovered home a good place to be and to bring his friends.

Joe is an example of thousands of middle adolescents —going from one form of recreation to the next—wanting something to do, yet not being satisfied with one thing, and in the process finding frustration and conflict.

In this day, when the boys do not need to chop wood and the girls do not need to hang out wash, the necessity for an outlet for their physical energies becomes doubly important. Growing muscles need activities. Expanding energies demand expression. Experimentation in recreation and the development of physical skills and mental co-ordination is imperative to youth's self-development and respect.

It is easy for youth to become spectators instead of participators in active sports. Private, rather than public, schools have the better record of physical fitness among students because they insist upon participation. In one study of flexibility tests given to grade and high school students, 52 per cent of high school graduates from public schools failed. From private schools, failure was only 14 per cent.*

Consistent exercise benefits children, youth, and adults. It tends to ease states of tension and fatigue, to reduce violent emotions, and contributes to weight control. Physical fitness increases enjoyment of work and play, encourages zest for new experiences, contributes to courage in tackling problems, and gives energy to do things of consequence. A fit person uses 20 per cent less energy for any move than does a flabby or weak person. Recreation is important.

Young people want and should have recreational opportunities with other young people in church fellowship. There are church leaders who look askance at church-sponsored ball, hockey, bowling, skiing, or physical fitness programs. Others have accepted the challenge of youth's need to actively participate in recreation within the fellowship of a Christian group. A

*Kraus report, 1956. Institute of Rehabilitation, N. Y. University.

youth leader can use the channels open to the youth group within his particular congregation for recreational activities. He may face the task of bridging the gap between the understandings of the older and younger members and finding outlets acceptable to those who are critical of youth's recreational needs.

He can guide youth as they choose from the variety of commercial recreation clamoring for their enthusiasm, money, participation. Programs planned to equip youth to judge the merits of individual forms of recreation are readily accepted by this age group. *Youth Program Ideas, 2* contains plans for four sessions dealing with recreation. They are entitled "Don't Miss the Fun." *Volume 3* includes suggestions for creative recreational activities under the title, "No Idle Moment." *Right or Wrong* deals with movies, dancing, gambling, and other problems.

Youth often want to know whether some one thing is right or wrong. They would rather the decision were made by someone else; then they could argue with it or find exceptions. Not all commercial recreation is detrimental, and it is often difficult for anyone to say what is wrong or right for another person because there are so many factors to consider.

Perhaps a more Biblical question to suggest for youth to ask themselves when they are in doubt about their recreational activities is: Is this beneficial to me as a Christian? This makes them look squarely at the factors that contribute to their spiritual growth and health, and analyze the affect of the recreation upon both body and mind.

Other questions that can help a youth group discuss recreation are:

1. How might this recreation improve my health or be a hazard?

2. Will this exhilarate me mentally? Or will it appeal to my passions?

3. Do the people who engage in this recreation symbolize my ideal of Christian living? How will associating with them influence me?

4. Does this amusement teach skills that could be used in objectionable ways? Does it teach me skills I will want to retain for life?

The youth leader can encourage group activities within the homes of the members of the youth fellowship. Why should not the homes or church youth center be a meeting place for Christian young people's social gatherings? To the farm home the matter of space should be no problem. But in urban homes living quarters are often limited. Even then there may be basement recreation rooms available for the cleaning and decorating, and often they are not being used because no one makes the effort to utilize the space. As mentioned before, when there is no adequate meeting place, then the possibility of turning an attic or basement, vacant garage, barn, or storage space into a youth center should be studied. It is not so much expensive entertainment and exclusive quarters that young people desire, but the privilege of associating with their friends where laughter and jokes and chatter aren't getting them into trouble with adults. A church-sponsored youth center, warm in winter and near outdoor cooking facilities in summer, can provide the hub around which a vigorous program for youth can be planned.

This is a fast-moving age; and unless the church, with its adult members, enters into a program that takes the recreational needs of its youth into consideration, the entertainment of the world will have a greater appeal. Every wage earner studies with care how he may improve his earning power, and this same effort should be expended for the success and happiness of youth and the homes they represent.

Youth leaders can also keep an eye open to ways to vary the social and recreational activities of their groups. Youth want diversity of activity—variety. For experimentation and gaining a backlog of experiences constitute an important part of learning. When repetition of games, crafts, sports, or recreational features becomes boring, it is past time to change the schedule. Public and church libraries can provide game books to relieve monotony in party games, and the four volumes of *Youth Program Ideas* have a variety of ideas for games, retreats, cookouts, outdoor worship services, and seasonal suggestions for stimulating activities.

Intellectual Characteristics

The middle adolescent seeks mental stimuli in many areas of thought and activity. He is susceptible to a wide range of intellectual materials. And where his formal education is inadequate, he may develop an avocation or hobby just because his interest keeps him reading, working, and exploring.

The reading craze gradually declines. For some, reading interests drop sharply while others maintain a steady reading program. This is due in part to the increased economic responsibility some adolescents assume and the need of others to begin to put into action the things they have read. Both boys and girls are taken up with a round of social activities and Christian service projects so that the amount of time left for reading is limited. For this age group, sharpening wits by talking with contemporaries is a chief intellectual exercise.

Youth of this period dream of ambition. They look at the future as a vast field to be conquered. In daring, they often tread ground that the aged and experienced fear to tread. They are self-styled critics, demanding that all argument be based on facts that stand the test of scientific data. Although they do work out things by degrees, their reasoning is not always logical. Their cocksure judgment gradually mellows as they discover that they make mistakes and that it is possible for them to be wrong.

Youth leaders can capitalize on youth's preoccupation with conversation, using techniques for learning that allow free exchange of opinions, findings, and ideas. Panel discussions, buzz sessions for small groups, reports, "my opinion" meetings, conducting polls, taking a census, formal debating, and informal chatting sessions all can serve acceptably as means for learning.

The middle adolescent's varied interests open up a vast assortment of topics to absorb his attention. To name just a few—human relations; personality development; personality problems; dating; current events and the Christian's responsibility; relation to government;

6

doctrines of the Bible; the Christian and war; church
history; hymnody; chorus; beliefs and traditions; conscience, culture, and group influence; meaning of
church membership; God and man's salvation; science
and the Bible; Bible history; how we got our Bible;
missions and relief; vocations and opportunities for
service within the church; handicrafts and skills; eti-
quette.

Spiritual Growth

Spiritually, young people of this age are vagabonds.
Many shift from defeat and failure to short-lived joy and
happiness, only to return again to defeat. Boys may
think churchgoing is sissy. Girls get weary of being good.
It is a period of spiritual bankruptcy, sacrilege, and dis-
respect. Middle teens tend to be irreverent, often skip-
ping church. They think of religion in terms of sermons,
baptism, ritual, and religious activity which they do not
connect with everyday life.

The young people themselves are aware of this problem. A seventeen-year-old said, "You have to go inwardly bankrupt to find God." Then questioning the logic
of his own reasoning, he added, "But there are people
who meet inward ruin and do not find God."

The young person this age is a pragmatist. He asks,
"Does this thing called religion work?" Frequently he
decides it does not. Paul, aged fifteen, reared in a Chris-
tion home, delivered his ultimatum when he was discovered neglecting his devotional life. "Last year," he
declared, "I prayed and made wretched grades. This
year I don't pray and my grades are much better. There
is nothing to religion." Immediate returns—that's what

the middle teener wants—whether in prayer or work. Clearly he is in transition from his early adolescent belief that Christ does everything in the life of the believer to the more mature concept that it is Christ dwelling within that enables the Christian to live a godly life.

This is part of the development toward a mature Christian faith—a part of the strong tendency for those who are converted in childhood or early adolescence to go through three stages of faith. *The first of these is the faith of the intellect.* It is the childlike simplicity that accepts all that has been taught about God and His Word. When the Spirit of God calls, these young people yield. They have a genuine experience of salvation—but their concept of the life in Christ is limited by their emotional, intellectual, and physical immaturity. And they soon discover that their vision of no defeats, no failures, no temptations is hardly reality.

As they grow older they experience alternate periods of being good and times of actual yielding to wrong. Then they may gradually shift to *the second stage—a faith of emotion.* During revival meetings or youth or missionary conference an adolescent's emotions may be touched. He decides that his life has not been fair to God, and he determines to do better and be more faithful. Hidden sin may be confessed and restitution made and once more he goes blissfully on. Later his emotions may cool and he is back where he was. When this happens a number of times, he begins to doubt, "Does this thing called religion really work in everyday life?" Perhaps he discusses his problem among friends and discovers they have some of the same doubts—perhaps he does not. But until he discovers answers to questions that plague him and shake his faith, he will be in spiritual turmoil.

Part of middle teen-agers' inner turmoil may be the result of a sharper discernment of right and wrong. For, as they have been walking in the light following conversion, they begin to sense imperfections in their lives as against the white light of Christ's righteousness. They may wonder and question, "Why can another Christian do something that my conscience won't allow?" They may finally say, "If that person can do it, I can too," and find themselves doing what they really believe is wrong.

Youth who continue doubtful practices cannot hope to grow. Whether they are experimenting with what they feel is wrong but other Christians do not—or whether they are continuing definitely unchristian attitudes and conduct—the result is the same. They are in conflict and doubts plague them.

How can I know I am saved? They may ask.

I do not feel I am saved. Am I?

How do I know God still loves me?

I thought I was saved, but now I don't know.

If I am saved, am I automatically born again? I don't always act as though I were.

An evil environment may corrode a Christian's faith. Drunkenness, quarreling, and family opposition to a decisive change may whittle away at the faith of a new Christian. The influence of the old gang may chisel its way through even a strong armor; and should a young Christian be forced to remain in his old environment, without sufficient sympathetic guidance and love to bulwark him from the inroads of evil, he may fall in the way.

Other environmental influences may heighten the middle adolescent's feelings of doubt and uncertainty about his experience of salvation. The modern, materialistically pagan home is not conducive to spiritual growth. For many parents the highest good is physical health, bodily pleasures and comforts, business success, and social prestige. Their happiness, it appears, is complete without God. It is hard for a young Christian to grow in such an atmosphere—where religion is a good thing but not necessarily to be worked at, or of serious implications.

But a third type of environment is by far the most subtly insidious. The setting is the Christian home where regular attendance at church and Sunday-school and communion is expected. The parents are active either in teaching or extension work, and deep in their hearts they appreciate the church—but the children have little way of knowing it. For on Sunday the pastor's message is criticized, and the Sunday-school superintendent's remarks are critically reviewed. Caustic remarks are made about the church finances and organization and leadership, and during the week Christian ethics are not known. The father may recommend a vicious kicker as a perfectly docile cow, and the mother may tell a friend she's had her wash out since eight, when really she had only one tub out at that hour. Such a distorted ethical standard makes religion seem a mockery to teen-agers.

But even when young people grow up in a satisfactory Christian environment and have received nurture that continues after conversion, they may face doubts in middle adolescence—in fact they are likely to. For a young life full of problems is a life that is awake. Jesus said, "Blessed are they which do hunger and thirst. . . ." When young people ask questions about the Christian life, they are demonstrating a spiritual appetite. They are seeking to grow in knowledge and understanding.

The many reasonable questions of adolescents are often about the Bible, as well as their own Christian experience. Public schools often present the theories of evolution and human progress, leaving the final matter up to the teen-ager. A chance remark by someone whom the teen-ager respects may set him to wondering about how the Bible came to be, and whether we can believe it. He may wonder why the Bible gives the impression that heaven is up—when anyone who lives in this age knows that space is out and out and out. Up is only relative. He may hear some ministers say that Jesus is coming back to this earth to reign as a King. Others may say that we cannot know exactly about the end of time—only that Christ has promised that where He is, there those who love Him will be also.

They ask:

Is the Bible true? Is it scientific?

What proof have we that the Bible is God-inspired and not the writings of men, if some people get one thing from it and others something else?

Was Jesus' claim to being divine valid, or was He mistaken?

Can you prove that there is a God?

Can we know that Jesus rose from the dead?

The middle adolescent, whose questions and spiritual problems are honestly received and answered, usually gains new ground in victory over sin. The process may be slow, but, when he looks back over twelve months of Christian experience, he will usually say that it is easier to forgive, to control anger, to return kindness for malice, to pray, and to read his Bible. Here is evidence of growing victory over the old nature, of growth toward the third stage of spiritual experience.

A new stage of spiritual experience is the acceptance of Christ as a matter of faith. It is the result of probing the above questions and discovering, after all the facts are in, that Christianity is something beyond reasoning which asks only to be accepted and acted on. It appeals to faith and obedience.

When the Christian accepts a truth by faith, the Spirit sets the seal of inner experience upon it. Then the knowledge that comes by faith is no longer hearsay, but proof from within. This is the dynamic of faith.

Young people in the throes of spiritual uncertainty put up walls of callous coldness or bluff indifference. Yet they want adults to surround them with an unshaken faith of their own. Secretly, they hope to be convinced that their doubts are wrong, and that they will awaken to the joy of a true Christian experience.

Youth leaders can accept the doubts of middle adolescents as a process of natural growth. Youth, too, when they realize that the years from fifteen to nineteen are often considered the great doubting years, are often relieved. That knowledge alone seems to open up their sources of understanding and allow them freedom to learn. Starbuck* discovered, in his study of the religious histories of many people, that 79 per cent of the men and 53 per cent of the women had periods of doubt in adolescence. Many of these were bitter struggles. These periods of doubt are as frequent in the lives of those well nurtured as in the lives of those poorly nurtured—perhaps more so, because they have more to doubt.

If young people are not guided through this period of doubts and skepticism to true faith, they may become indifferent and be lost to a living faith in Christ.

Guidance involves, first of all, letting youth express all their misgivings, questions, and doubts. Questioning is at the very basis of man's ability to learn. Until a person wants an answer—that answer, no matter how cleverly given and interestingly presented, may affect him very little. But when the desire to know stirs the mind to wonder and exploration, the stage is set for effective learning.

Guidance includes supplying source books of the facts and of knowing the facts. In the past, religious leaders have often been content to pass on generalities and dogmas. But young people respect evidence and facts. Their intelligence demands honesty if their searching minds are to arrive at faith. Youth need the facts about how our Bible came to us. They need to know the findings of Bible scholars, historians, and archaeologists. They need to know the history of the Bible's translation and the stories of those translators.

*Starbuck, Edwin, *Psychology of Religion.*

They need to see Jesus in the land where He lived. They need to see Him as the person His followers knew Him to be. They need to follow the spread of Christianity from its small home in Palestine to the whole of the Roman Empire, and subsequently north and west to Europe and the West.

The middle adolescent needs to become a vital participant in the church. To be this he must be able to say, "I know whom I have believed," not because the pastor has said it, or parents have believed it, but because he has experienced it in his own heart. His "I know" must include understanding of how salvation was enacted for him, and confession of the heart that can say to these truths, "I believe," and know where to find them in the Scriptures.

Jesus Christ is the Son of God. John 1:18.

Jesus left glory to die for us, that believing we might have life. I Cor. 15:3.

Jesus rose from the dead, that we too may have power over sin. Eph. 1:19, 20.

Jesus is with the Father interceding in our behalf. Heb. 7:25.

Jesus is my personal Redeemer. John 3:16.

In addition, if a young person is to become an intelligent member of his home congregation, he must clearly understand the local program and be a participant in it. Pastors, superintendents, Sunday-school teachers, and youth leaders can stimulate curiosity and eager participation. They can invite and welcome middle teen-agers to congregational business meetings; they can ask the youth fellowship to elect a representative to the educational council of the church. Youth can be expected to report on their youth organization at the annual church business meeting. And they can be invited to observe the work of the church council at one of its sessions.

Youth leaders can suggest that the youth fellowship invite the chairman of the church council and the church board to explain the work of their boards to the young people. Youth can study their church's constitution, its organization, committees, government, business arrangements, and total program of education, evangelism, outreach, and service.

In addition, each young person should be aware of the relationship of his congregation to the larger denominational organization. Attending district conference sessions, meetings of general conference, and publication and mission board meetings can broaden their experiences with other youth of their denomination, and, yet at the same time, give them a vision of the scope of work of their denomination.

But the ideal church is not the real church. Young people must not be shielded from the weaknesses of the church. They must know God's work is done by men and women who are human and have failure and defeat to face at times, just as younger people have. Youth leaders' mature attitudes will influence youth to see that men who fail at times, or who seem to them to have blind spots, can still be God's instruments to carry out His will.

Youth leaders can also aid in the development of mature faith and meaningful membership within the

denomination, by providing summer Bible school classes for this age group. Often, part or full-time jobs do
not allow youth to attend morning or afternoon classes,
and those who could attend are asked to serve as helpers or teachers in the preschool and primary depart-
ments. Thus teen-agers are denied the advantages of
two weeks of concentrated Bible study at the very time
they are troubled by questions about their relationship
to God, and about the history and authenticity of the
Bible. Many churches have solved this problem by ar-
ranging for evening classes during the two weeks Bible
school is in process, or at another suitable time.

Special weekend conferences and workshops, and ongoing weekly meetings can serve the same purpose—but
with lesser results. Some materials available for concentrated study are: *Getting Acquainted with the Old Testament, Getting Acquainted with the New Testament,
The Bible Speaks to You, Ways Youth Learn,* and *A
Spiritual Clinic.*

A most important single help is a modern version of
the Bible. There are many fine ones available, perhaps
the most used of which is the Revised Standard Version.
But Moffatt and Williams are good, as are also Wey-
mouth and Phillips. Phillips' *Letters to Young Churches*
is available in a paper cover edition and is especially
helpful to understanding the epistles of the New Testament.

The King James, with its archaic beauty, has made
many present-day Christians think that the Bible is a
book with a special religious language. In reality, the
Bible was written not in the classical language of its day

but in the common speech of the people to whom it was directed. When the King James version was made, back in the seventeenth century, the language used in it was the ordinary speech of the times. Today it sounds formal, for languages change; words gather new meanings and lose their old ones. Therefore, if the Bible is to remain fresh and meaningful for each generation, new translations will always be necessary.

Searching youth, who discover the true significance of the Bible, will develop a high respect for the truth.

They want to read the Bible to discover its meaning for them—to unearth the words of Jesus that cast light upon the path they are walking. They grow from the stage of feeling they should read the Bible because they've been told they should to the level of maturity that seeks the transformation of their wills as they learn of God through the Scriptures.

Youth may misunderstand spiritual growth even while growing. They may want to take the virtues of Christ one by one and emulate them. Youth leaders help them take an important step forward when they teach and live that growing in the Christian life is rather making Jesus Lord and Master of their total personalities. Then fears, ambitions, perplexities, inquiries, passions, feelings, secret longings, and attitudes and actions are considered matters for His control.

Paul strongly commands the Romans to "put on the Lord Jesus Christ, and make no provision for the flesh" (Rom. 13:14). This is a continuing process, for youth, who are passing through the second stage in the maturation of faith, often have difficulty breaking with worldly associates who cannot be influenced to become Christians. Adopting new modes of recreation when the old are disintegrative and harmful, and using good English instead of slang are details that take time. Making Christ Lord is not easy. It also involves matters that lie deep within the personality of youth: changing thought patterns, giving service instead of feeding pride, learning to discuss instead of argue, and to count another's joy more important than one's own.

Growing youth need encouragement and stimulation, for they are learning that growth requires effort—even though it does not result alone from study and concentration. But when youth eagerly read their Bibles, readily confess their faults and sins, seek and accept God's constant forgiveness, and in thanksgiving obey His guidance, they are appropriating the power of His Spirit that indwells them. They are moving toward spiritual maturity.

Chapter 4

Later Adolescence
Years 18 to 24

THE LATER adolescent is near adulthood. The twenty-one-year-old girl knows that she has made a marked change since her eighteenth year. Likewise, the seventeen-year-old boy does not feel a part of the world of his brother who is twenty. The early part of later adolescence is akin to middle adolescence just as the latter part of adolescence is similar to adulthood. This period, as others, indicates growth.

Early adolescence was marked by conflict and change; middle adolescence by crises and problems; later adolescence is generally characterized as a period of reconstruction or reorganization.

Physical Maturity

Nature has foreseen that greater needs than physical growth should be attended to in this almost-mature period. The later adolescent is no longer fearful of his body, for it is no longer all out of proportion. The boy uses his voice with greater modulation. And although he may add a little weight and height after twenty, his growth is practically complete. But the development of power, skill, and the capacity of endurance may continue until senescence sets in.

The young woman is less aware of herself than in the two preceding periods. She is more conscious of herself as an individual in possession of ideas, personality, skill, and efficiency. The young man's physical energy, needed earlier for growth, is now channeled into activity and the development of strength. This is the period when great athletes are developed, feats demanding endurance are tried, and pioneering has appeal. In young women, the physical vigor is similar—especially in the achieving of work that brings satisfaction in an aesthetic and spiritual way. Women show less interest, however, in participating in athletics. Their activity takes a social turn. And women this age feel an urge to get things done.

Both men and women have splendid equipment for work. Health, morale, interest, and ambition run high. Frequently, young people do not appreciate the close relationship between good health and efficiency, nor that health affects success in all undertakings—personal and social. A healthy body works as an integrated whole, ticking not on eight or twelve cylinders—but on all of the thirty-three trillion cells. Many young people experience this harmonious working of their bodies, but many never realize their physical potential and are not aware of their loss. Some are not responsible for ill health; others are partially handicapped in success and happiness because they fail to follow rules of simple, intelligent, sensible living.

Young people easily forget that health cannot be squandered and at the same time preserved. They'd rather burn the candle at both ends than not burn it at all. Then they like to take a weekend to catch up on sleep, hoping the reservoir will fill up as they rest. But sometimes their prodigal spending of energy stirs up troubles they hadn't expected: fatigue on the job, sniffles, stomach upsets, and no end of minor ailments. Later adolescents are apt to schedule their week nights so full that they often are not at their best for a special date or trip, excursion or conference that they had looked forward to for weeks.

When later youth discover that the stewardship of health is a means of service to humanity, as well as the means to attain personal goals, they have begun to live intelligently and maturely.

Later adolescents must be reminded that health is more than freedom from illness and disorder; it is an abundance of life. They need the casual humor of the adult counselor to remind them of the hour for adjournment of committee meetings. They need the youth leader's assistance to help them stick by hours they have set for coming in from dates, youth fellowship meetings, parties, etc.

Because their reserve of energy is great, young people are often given more responsibility and work than they can adequately handle in their leisure time. Later adolescents are vulnerable at this point, because they will go until they are exhausted. Then youth leaders may observe that details are being overlooked, plans are only half-formulated, or an important meeting is poorly attended. They will see beyond techniques and procedures and the delegating of authority, and perhaps suggest the adjustment of the work loads of those who hold places of responsibility within the youth fellowship group.

EMOTIONAL MATURITY

When the twelve-month-old child pounds his spoon on his small plate and screams for food, no one is alarmed. But if the six-year-old manifests the same conduct, we might be tempted to say he is either spoiled or abnormal. If the six-year-old says to a visitor, "See my new shoes," it may be a little embarrassing to the parent, but not too serious. But should the twelve-year-old do the same, it is a different matter. The twelve-year-old's door-slamming is certainly not desirable; nevertheless, it may be a little in keeping with some of his other actions. But if the eighteen-year-old indulges in such emotional upheavals, it is a matter about which to be concerned. If the eighteen-year-old engages in light little acts of social jollity to gain the attention of the opposite sex, we do not accuse him too much; but such actions by a thirty-year-old would be looked on with askance. Thus we expect different levels of maturity.

Emotional maturity is not a state of personality achieved overnight. It is gained gradually. Fortunate is the youth who, throughout childhood, has had those about him whose actions resulted from mature emotions, and who could intelligently guide him into ways

7

of reacting that were both satisfactory and suitable to his age.

The middle adolescent, bridging the chasm between childhood and adulthood, often blunders. Feelings that were smoldering throughout childhood, now burst into flame. His conduct is based on his feelings, and he exhibits strong likes and dislikes. His feelings come into play in making decisions, ways of meeting people, approaches to activities, and interpretation of worship experiences. Feeling is the expression of human emotion, and the middle adolescent seems at times to be all emotion—acting out his every feeling.

But middle adolescents want to be mature. About this, also, they feel strongly. And this becomes the first step in the process of gaining control over their feelings. By eighteen, adolescents are well on the way to understanding that they need not be at the mercy of their emotional feelings, but they can direct these energies into worth-while activities.

They discover that their feelings are effective in clinching a learning experience. All real learning involves experience of some kind, either vicarious or direct. The effectiveness of the learning experience is influenced by the emotional content accompanying it. A youth who accidentally wrecks his father's car will go through an emotional learning experience—about caution, police, insurance, and injured.

His emotions also make worship meaningful. Feelings of warmth, awe, reverence, majesty, love, and repentance assist the adolescent's maturing sense of fellowship with God.

The driving power that brings him to success or failure is also furnished by his emotions. Much that he experiences either affects his immediate actions or is pushed into the unconscious areas of his personality. No experience is actually lost in the effect it has on the individual. Younger adolescents tend to relegate to their unconscious minds the issues surrounding conflicts and the other unpleasant things of their lives. But later adolescents want to diagnose their problems and seek solutions within the limitations of which they are aware. And at this age they can be inspired to habits of intelligent action; for they are willing to face problems, learn to take them apart—root and all—and plan a course of action for their solution, foreseeing the results of this action.

Because later adolescents are less afraid to face new situations, they are willing to welcome new points of view with a view to discovering the facts. If necessary, they are willing to change their ways of thinking and acting. Although they are less free to speak their own opinions, they are more eager to get the opinions of others. On the whole, later adolescents are better listeners. They are ready to acknowledge mistakes and do not resent honest criticism. This changing of opinions about something they have long disbelieved or believed is, for many, one of the most difficult steps in the process of maturing; for prejudices have a viselike grip on many people—both young and old.

Later adolescents are emotionally able to change behavior patterns, because now they can understand that this is not mature or childish, but a sign of enlarged ability to face new situations, and to employ creativity in devising new methods of behavior. This is the substance pioneers are made of.

Mature youth are learning to face failures and accept disappointment. They are able to look on them almost philosophically, sensing that into each life comes some failure, some disappointment. They realize that the world remembers more kindly those who succeed, not because they encounter few difficulties, but because they use the difficulties as steppingstones to success.

Youth this age are also able to be fair to themselves in making an estimate of their abilities and limitations. This is important because it affects their attitude toward their vocation and service. Nearly all adolescents shrink from assuming responsibility, but an honest evaluation of their capacities, aptitudes, and preferences boosts their self-confidence and assists them toward a healthy acceptance of the fact that they must carry their share of the world's work.

Another evidence of the maturation of the emotions of older adolescents is a growing ability to understand others. Many young people in their early twenties not only discover themselves, but also learn many of the magic secrets of working and living happily with others. This is more maturing of their emotions than the maturing of their social nature. Self-understanding opens up mainsprings of broader understanding, and those who understand themselves are more likely to understand others.

As they become more appreciative and understanding of others, their fear disappears, as does also their self-assertiveness and boasting. Courage is gained out of the knowledge that satisfactory relationships have been established. Thus confidence is gradually built up, and service to others is possible.

Thus the maturation of his emotions allows the average normal later adolescent to react to life with a rising sense of security, to have a reasonable attitude toward social mores, to assume responsibility whatever praise or blame it entails, to develop sensitivity to values, and to make decisions on the basis of quality or worth, right or wrong.

SOCIAL RELATIONSHIPS

The later adolescent period gives rise to a growing social self-consciousness. The personal life of youth begins to narrow and deepen, but in the wider areas of employment, home life, worship, and service to humanity, his relationships to others broaden. "I'm tired of making money; it isn't everything," remarked a young woman who had been thrust on her own, economically, early in life. Later adolescence awakened her spiritual and social sense of responsibility toward others. Her outlook on life broadened. She wanted to explore the possibilities for service to others, and she finally chose a type of service in which the possibilities to serve others in the name of Christ were limitless.

This young woman could symbolize her age group. The sacrificial spirit of early adolescence is tempered by reason and experience. Altruism is not a vague and dreamy ideal, but an impelling force that pushes later adolescents into pioneering projects. The quality of these relationships with others varies with the wide range of individual backgrounds: individual differences in temperament, capacities, interests, ability to obtain what they desire, and power to influence others. Much work in the church and in mission has been done by young people before they have entirely reached adulthood. Others have completed in maturity the tasks they envisioned in later adolescence.

Their ripening social sense also leads later adolescents to organizing. This drive has led to the founding of many youth organizations. So strong is this urge that where adults have not led in organizing young people, adolescents have created organizations either to their own credit or harm.

The gang or the group, which formed the social unit outside the home for middle adolescents, gives way to individuality as youth become less and less interested in themselves as physical persons. Girls no longer need to identify with the group by following fads. They are conscious of how the style and color of their clothing enhance their features, coloring, and figures. Fellows spend much time grooming to impress the opposite sex, and make a bid for attention. They find personal satisfaction in excelling in athletics, purchasing and caring for fine cars, obtaining good jobs—or whatever the standard of success among the youth of their community.

Later adolescence may easily be called the period of romance. The heroes and heroines of fiction are invariably of this age. The sex repulsion of early adolescence and the superficial impulsive love affairs of middle adolescence are superseded by a more significant and lasting attraction between the sexes. Friendships narrow as the universal impulse of love between the sexes seeks fruition.

By later adolescence young people have a rather well-developed mental image of their ideal marriage partner. When someone suddenly appears who by outward appearance fulfills that ideal, something clicks and young people may think that they have fallen in love. This love at first sight they often discover to be a one-sided infatuation. But it is not impossible for the relationship to ripen into true love, as these young people—who only recently were strangers—over a period of time and association, shift from love of ideal to love of person.

Older adolescents are less inclined to rush in and out of love affairs than their younger siblings. Feeling less need to act sophisticated and grownup, because they are more mature, they are more likely to take their time. In our culture, most of the responsibility of choice rests with the youth themselves. Therefore, a considerable period of time is required for acquaintance and social ease to develop—through association in varied circumstances—so that young people can learn to know and love one person sufficiently for marriage.

But later adolescents are often tempted to court physically rather than intellectually or socially. Their physical drives are strong and still new, pushing for expression. This desire to express sexual passion sometimes drives young people into heavy petting and premarital love affairs, leaving them with guilt feelings and a pattern of courting that is difficult to by-pass when they seek to initiate another friendship.

Some youth find religious taboos and fear adequate to guard their premarital chastity. Others who are aware that medical technology has reduced fear of the unfortunate consequences of intercourse, and lessened the possibility of discovery and disgrace, will seek personal and social values of a positive nature. These young people find, in the ethic of love and character, a resource for standards of sexual behavior. As they put the welfare and highest good, both of their friends and themselves, above temporary personal pleasure, they achieve genuine personal satisfaction and a rewarding social relationship.

Others discover that a friendship based on physical attraction alone does not allow them to share the many other interesting parts of their personalities. They sense that a friendship based on petting is really not a friendship, for the interest in each other is purely biological. They find the distinctiveness of their individuality is sacrificed when they are preoccupied with only one aspect of personality. Excessive physical contact short-circuits friendships, so that other qualities cannot be expressed. Young people who learn that love comes slowly, but more securely, on the wings of honor and self-respect and high esteem of one's friends, have learned a wonderful truth to hold them in good stead in times of stress.

Most later adolescents want to be realistic about their love affairs. They each want theirs to be marriage that lasts a lifetime. They learn from experience that love is not all moonlight and roses, and they want to consider all the factors that might influence marriage either for better or worse. They desire help in discovering the basis for mutuality, in deciding whether theirs is really the real thing, in evaluating their family backgrounds and religious orientation, in working out the problems of advance education, delayed marriage or parenthood, and finances.

Mature youth need to be given as much responsibility as they are able to handle in planning and organizing the youth activities of their age group. Adult sponsorship and guidance should not stand in the way of their planning and executing the program of activities, socials, and formal sessions that meet their felt needs.

Often later adolescents can be used to organize early adolescent clubs, the junior-hi group, under the direction of the youth leader. They can be camp counselors, craft and recreation specialists, nature enthusiasts, and efficient class instructors in well-directed junior and junior-hi camps.

Youth leaders can assist the Sunday-school superintendent and department superintendents in choosing teachers from this age group. Girls can direct chapters of their group, and boys can head junior boys' clubs. Often youth this age are capable of directing choruses; organizing quartets, ensembles, mixed octets; and planning speaking teams for special purposes.

Denominational service committees gladly keep youth leaders informed of service opportunities for mature youth. Both summer and year-around projects—from hospital service to summer Bible schools in migrant camps—are planned to attract persons of varied interests. Youth leaders can pass this information on and encourage later adolescents to volunteer for service—either short- or long-term.

Youth leaders can help mature adolescents both directly and indirectly with their romances. Conferences planned for mature youth—and limited to them—can open up discussions never possible in groups monopolized by adults and younger teens. Here, in a limited conference, speakers and discussion leaders can be asked to speak beyond the usual generalities and platitudes and probe the questions youth ask: How can I protect myself from giving affection to the wrong person? How can I know when it is true love? How can I prepare myself to make a good sex adjustment in marriage? How can engagement help me toward a good marriage? Why should we wait for a mere license and public ceremony? Should I marry outside my religion?

Small study groups can tackle reading and can discuss together books such as these whose purpose is to help mature youth prepare for successful marriage: *Marriage for Moderns, When You Marry, Marriage, The Art of Lasting Love, Too Young to Marry, If I Marry Outside My Religion, Good Housekeeping Marriage Book.* (See bibliography at the end of this book.)

Indirectly a youth leader may influence the marriage ideals and attitudes of mature youth by inviting them into his home for informal music, games, and discussion. Seeing a young family in operation—sharing joys and sacrificing short-term satisfactions for longer-term goals—can inspire young adults to wholesome thought about what really matters in a marriage.

When a youth leader sees that an individual is not

finding satisfying association among the youth of the church group, he can encourage that individual to find employment in another community, to continue schooling, or to choose voluntary service, where the possibilities for friendship are more encouraging.

Sometimes those who seem unable to establish satisfactory friendships with others of the opposite sex need to be given opportunities to express their love by working with children or in group projects. They may need understanding of their shyness or particular personality problem and welcome the counsel of the youth leader who should be ready to listen and guide them into a solution of their particular problem. Books to aid the youth leader in counseling are suggested in the bibliography (see page 153).

Intellectual Pursuits

In later teens and early twenties youth begin to formulate concepts of the meaning of life. Experience aids their seeing relative values, for they have begun to train their minds to observe human nature, to ask questions about what they don't know, to find solutions to problems, to discover the meanings of their feelings, and to let new ideas challenge their imaginations.

Their mental maturity can be measured by their attitudes toward intellectual growth, and their ability to evaluate social relationships, to see situations as a whole, to interpret experiences as meaningful learnings for the future, and to follow scientific processes in arriving at solutions to problems.

Youth whose formal education stops with elementary

grades often spends little time in individual personal study during these years. For many of this group the demands of labor seem great, and leisure time is used for recreation. Those who enter college pass into a category that is often outside the influence of the youth leader. For these the main purpose of their efforts for the later adolescent years is intellectual development and vocational preparedness. The largest group, those who finish high school and become job seekers, are certain to acquire knowledge and experience also that can enlarge their intellectual outlook. Many do read, the majority preferring fiction. Poetry, scientific books, and biography are also on their lists. Magazines of the more serious type are preferred by the industrial group.

"How long shall we continue to study?" many young people this age ask. Some look back and sigh with regret that their days in the schoolroom were limited to a few years of formal education. Others in graduating from high school say, "My school days are over; my days of study are past, and that is that." Glad to be relieved of the necessity for study, later adolescents may stumble into a rut of reading very little serious material, even failing to keep alert to advancements, changes in techniques, and discoveries in their own vocational field. Such habits are not unusual, for there are many who fail to realize that opportunity favors the trained mind. It does not ask primarily how this trained mind gained its skill or understanding. It accepts those who think and act and grow intellectually. It wants the educated youth who understands, knows to do and does, and whose mind is always open to new learning.

Later adolescents who miss out on high school often have little opportunity for units of study on straight thinking and problem solving that could correct these misunderstandings about education. Others are glad to review their learnings and to rethink the difficulties they encounter in today's world when they want to think straight.

A youth leader stands in a strategic position to help later adolescents to want to grow intellectually. He is aware of the many possibilities for educational improvement available today, and can direct the young person whether his interests are industrial, cultural, philosophical, or recreational.

The youth leader should know the offerings of church colleges. He should be on the mailing lists of these schools so that he is kept informed of development programs and changes and additions to curriculums, and he should be able to suggest the name of the person at each school to whom the interested youth could write for additional information. Thus the youth leader can function as a liaison for church colleges and youth.

There are all sorts of additional possibilities for advanced education: night schools, correspondence courses, professional schools, trade schools, seminaries and universities, winter Bible schools, workshops, and radio and TV courses. In addition, young people can be introduced to and encouraged to visit industries, attend concerts and public lectures, travel to places of natural and historical interest, and plan study units on topics that intrigue them. Small groups of later adolescents have successfully formed clubs to learn a foreign language, add a skill such as typing, or develop an interest such as swimming and lifesaving, or scouting and camping.

Youth leaders can encourage young adults-to-be to read. Every young person should buy no less than six books a year, chosen on the basis of quality, interest, and permanent worth to the reader. By the time a young person is twenty-four he should have acquired approximately sixty to one hundred books, and be subscribing to at least one magazine yearly.

To encourage good reading habits, a youth leader can suggest that the youth organization of his church invite the church librarian to keep them up to date on new additions, and he can solicit suggestions for new purchases. If the group needs a review of books within the library, he can plan with the youth programing committee some suitable means of presenting these to the group.

The wide-awake youth leader can stimulate later adolescents to sample books about many different subjects by sharing current purchases he has made and showing interest in the books the members of the group are buying and reading. He can also suggest that they invite the librarian of the school, the public library, or their church, to speak on how to judge the value of a book.

A youth group can in addition sponsor a tour of the public library and ask the librarian to give them a brief talk on library science: how to get the most a library has to offer.

Youth leaders can keep abreast of current publications in the field of youth interests. They can ask librarians of school and public libraries to keep them informed of new, good books; and they should remember to scan the book review sections of magazines, newspapers, and journals.

Films are another wonderful means of increasing one's experience and knowledge. Public libraries often feature a film-rental service and have a file of catalogs of new and old film productions available to local groups. Some of these are practically cost free, and are produced either in the interest of public welfare, safety, health, etc., or by corporations who use the films as a means of advertising.

The Mennonite Publishing House offers a review service on films for use by religious groups. This is available at a nominal price, and every youth group should have access to it.

Youth groups who have become interested in the books published by their denomination have profitably visited their publishing headquarters to see firsthand how books are chosen for publication, prepared, printed, and distributed.

By stimulating young people to read books on the same theme, or to suggest one particular book for the group to read, a youth leader can measurably increase the value of reading. In addition to introducing them to new thought, he has given them a common fund of knowledge which can in turn become the basis for discussion.

Young people also need to be helped to think creatively and to solve their problems logically if they are to mature intellectually. "The Why and How of Thinking," in the final chapter of this book, briefly presents why people think, how they can use their minds to solve problems and think creatively, and how they may avoid the pitfalls of faulty thought. It could form the basis of a series of programs designed to aid later adolescents to use their minds to the greatest possible advantage.

WORK AND VOCATION

Early and middle adolescents do not cheerfully accept work. One adroit wit has said, "Doubtless so many children are lazy because they are related to their parents." But by the time they reach later adolescence, young people have begun to gain a sense of the dignity of toil and to feel a certainty about becoming a participant in the workaday world.

Youth sense that labor can contribute to a significant cause, and they expect to achieve a measure of skill and success in a vocation. They anticipate some appreciation for the work they will do. Christian young people do not want to become like prisoners at a rock pile, ill-fitted to a job, or be plagued by a feeling that they have missed their work, by the hand of providence. They want to serve under the guidance of God's ever-present Spirit. Mature youth want to avoid these vocational problems. They do not want to lose their initiative and efficiency, their spark of creativity, by being ill-mated to a vocation. Therefore they wonder: first, whether a Christian must do full-time service to be in the will of the Lord, and they wonder, second, how to choose a vocation.

Christian youth look to the church and its youth leaders to help them answer these questions. Their seeking minds and positive attitudes toward success make later adolescents particularly open to vocational guidance. Youth do not think of the future in terms of failure, and remain undaunted in the face of tremendous odds —if they are certain of the right road and direction.

Youth leaders can become acquainted with resource materials to suggest when later adolescents may want to work out study units on vocation. They can be prepared to refer inquirers to sources of vocational guidance materials. The following books on vocations are recommended by G. Curtis Jones, author of *Youth Deserves to Know: Christian Youth and Christian Vocation, Careers for You, What Are You Doing? Young Christians at Work, Unfinished Business, Christian Faith and My Job, Work and Vocation, The Christian Answer.* (See the listing at the end of this book.)

"How to Find a Life Vocation," in the final chapter of this book, provides possible outlines for programs on the theme, "Aids to Finding God's Vocational Plan."

"Hearing the Call of a Church Vocation" presents a discussion of vocational opportunities within the church, qualifications for these jobs, and how God calls. This, too, is designed for use as program resource material.

SPIRITUAL CROSSROADS

The later adolescent is attracted by the appeals of two opposite centers of devotion. The one is a highly personalized faith in a transcendent God. It promises abiding fellowship with Christ. It offers the guidance of a divine

Spirit. It claims the unquestioned right to an individual's mental, physical, and spiritual powers. This is the God-centered appeal.

The other attraction sets up man as sovereign, claiming he is not in need of divine assistance to achieve the higher life. Within reasonable limits, he is able to attain his ideals by virtue of will power. He is responsible to his fellow men only, insomuch as his contribution to his neighbor will make his neighbor a better member of society. Otherwise life lays no claim on him. He is free to take the road to personal aggrandizement. This is the man-centered appeal.

Ultimately, all youth stand at the crossroads of decision. Shall it be the God-centered or the man-centered life? The adolescent between eighteen and twenty-four faces this choice more acutely than at any other age. He has outgrown the faith of his childhood. His concepts of God are no longer physical and external. God, whom he had earlier thought of as a man with a big book, or as a fatherly friend or a big policeman, is becoming an ever-present, inner Spirit, as well as a Sovereign. This transition from a childhood faith, to one that is personal and internal, is not easy for many a youth. With the expanding powers of his intellect, he seeks for rational answers to the supernatural in the tenets of his faith. He seeks to believe from his heart the tenets he earlier accepted as orthodox truth. But not until he has thought through his beliefs, and accepted them from his innermost being, is the truth really his own. His very nature craves for a strong consciousness of spiritual fellowship with God.

Here youth stands at the parting of the way. How each will decide depends largely upon his earlier inner experience, and the spiritual warmth, concern, and understanding he has received. It is a sad commentary to the Christian church that many young people either entirely drift away from the church or never experience a deep and satisfying relationship with Jesus Christ. The environmental influences for worldliness are wide and strong. Ideals that come from associations in public high schools often sow seeds of distrust, plant roots of indifference, and develop strong distaste for righteousness. These bear fruit in later adolescence. In addition, many popular recreations are utterly worldly and make thrusts at sacred institutions such as the home and the church.

The young person of this age is awakening. When the home and church capture his awakening soul after his siege of doubt and indecisions, he is saved to a life of devotion and service. When the demands of the world are stronger, he chooses the man-centered life. His future may be lost in materialism, indifference, agnosticism, or even atheism. Ultimately, his life will be service to self. What youth desires, before stepping out into this cold strata of reasoning, is someone to show him by wise guidance and personal example that the Christian way of life can be applied to everyday life. He wants to be shown—more than told—that Christianity is practical and will bring order into a life of chaos, and that one may know, feel, and live in God's presence.

Three types of youth in this age group present the

church with a tremendous challenge. First there are those who live beyond the pale of Christian influence and environment. Multitudes of these have never heard the story of salvation. Much less do they know of the beauty of a life in Christ. They need the Gospel message.

Second is a smaller group, who through parental guidance are brought to the Sunday school. Many or most of these become regular attendants, experience a deeper sense of need, and yield to the appeal of the Gospel. To these, the church and the Christian home render a real spiritual service. But, because of lack of aggressive teaching in the church or carnal Christian living in the home, many drift away from the deep current of spiritual life. Their lives lose the strength of a personal testimony, and spiritual fruit is not forthcoming.

The third group is the smallest by far. It consists of young people who have awakened to their true privileges in Christ. Their lives are Spirit-empowered. They see themselves a part of the living organism, the church. They see the church not only as an institution from which to obtain help and inspiration, but also as the avenue through which they offer their lives for service to Christ. They gain vitality from a close and vital relationship with Christ and the church. In this group lies the spiritual hope of the future. The challenge to the church is to bring as many as possible from the other groups into this level of spiritual life.

Some Pitfalls

Some of the pitfalls that ensnare later adolescent Christians in the second and third types listed above, and that keep them from maturing in their Christian experiences are given here:

Thinking their problems are different from those of other Christians. Although spiritual problems tend to be similar, the fear of being abnormal gives young people a very serious sense of aloneness that often keeps them from seeking spiritual counsel, drives them into despair, and prevents their being victorious in their Christian lives. It is often a balm to their troubled souls to discover that Christ was "in all points tempted like as we are, yet without sin" (Hebrews 4:15). Reading biographies of men and women of God helps them discover that even the great in Christ's kingdom have experiences similar to theirs.

Discrediting the church or congregation that led them to spiritual birth. Occasionally, during a plateau of spiritual inactivity, young people come under the influence of a new spiritual force. As new light dawns, they experience a deepening of their fellowship with God. Then, looking back over their lives, they may decide that the church or congregation most responsible for their spiritual welfare has been devoid of the truth or spirituality. And they may be swept away by the new influence, so that they can no longer be of service to the denomination or congregation which may be very greatly in need of their life, talent, and testimony.

Feeling that pastors preach the life of victory only as an ideal. Many young people do not believe victory is possible to attain—nor that ministers and youth leaders themselves experience it. Perhaps this is occasioned by the fact that many messages are not slanted to youth's experiences. Great truths, couched in traditional, flowery, or theological language, are not understood by youth. Justification, glorification, grace, and sanctification are terms that carry little meaning unless illustrated in simple words.

Not giving God credit for divine intervention in the everyday affairs of their lives. Young Christians often ignore the many occasions in which the hand of the Lord can be seen. They call their good fortune "luck," or they credit their own wisdom and intelligence. Failing to read God into important or minor events displays a subtle type of worldliness that honors self. God doubly blesses those who honor Him in a moment-by-moment recognition of His presence.

Hanging on to unconfessed sin until their souls become barren. Often the sins of youth are very minor and could be taken care of in a few minutes, but they become major issues because youth fear to confess them. Then they carry guilt feelings with them until they are driven almost to despair.

Neglecting private worship. Youth, who have been buoyed up and carried along in the surge of a spiritual experience in early or middle adolescence, may be tempted to reason that they are not quite so much in need of reading their Bibles and praying.

Often, when young people attend meetings of fellowship with other Christians, they feel it is not essential that they have private worship. Public religious meetings, they reason, will give them the needed spiritual food for their lives; and they fail to realize that inner resources, obtained from private worship, are their greatest strength for victory.

Worshiping the spiritual experience instead of worshiping Christ. At times the deepening of spiritual experience may become a very real pitfall to persons who spend too much time looking back to the experience— thinking and talking about it, and thanking God for it. But they never really enter into the fullness with Christ that God intended, because Satan subtly sidetracks them to thoughts of themselves and the experience.

Allowing victories to become a snare. Sometimes after young people have lived in defeat and suddenly learn victory, they fall worse than before. Satan attacks them on a different level, and may trip them into yielding to self-righteousness.

Glorifying an individual who helped them solve a problem. Youth's hero worship may cripple spiritual growth when it develops into an unwholesome situation where too great an attachment is involved.

Failing to make a thorough job of restitution. Sometimes, after confessing to a friend or leader the sins hidden in their hearts, youth delay making apologies, restoring things, or asking forgiveness. Often they will faithfully clear up all but one matter. This, Satan argues, is not important; and because they have appeased their consciences almost to the last point, and feel greatly unburdened, they listen to Satan's reasoning and venture forth. But they are not able to live victoriously because they are already defeated.

Lying concerning the Spirit's witness in their lives. This takes form in a multitude of ways. A common and serious way is that of giving an expression of peace when there is no peace. More serious yet is evading the issue, so that the lie need not be spoken, pretending to be honest by silence, but outwardly expressing the act of peace in sharing communion. This double hypocrisy is more prevalent in the lives of young people than is recognized. It could partially be remedied by helping young people feel free to come to youth leaders to make confession or establish understanding.

How to bring young Christians to this deeper experience is indeed a problem for parents and leaders. That many young people do not attain fullness in Christ is obvious. Perhaps it is because Christian youth leaders do not sufficiently explain the Spirit's work to young people. Perhaps it is because leaders are oblivious to the pitfalls mentioned previously and fail to guide and encourage youth when they are at spiritual crossroads.

It may be helpful for Christian youth leaders to recognize that young people are ready for a deeper Christian experience when the following circumstances are evident:

Living a life of alternating defeat and victory. This up-and-down type of Christian experience often precedes a consciousness that in the life of self there dwells no good thing.

Active in serving, but sensing little power. Young people, placed in positions of responsibility in the work of the Lord, may expend a great deal of effort, and yet sense that their labor fails to produce genuine victory either in their own lives or those of others. This may lead them to realize the need for a deeper Christian life.

One way to help young people to a deeper, more victorious experience is to study the subject with them. "How to Live Victoriously," in the final chapter, is designed to help youth leaders develop an outline and discussion guide for leading young people to an understanding of Christian victory.

"How to Recognize the Spirit," in the same chapter suggests a discussion of victorious living, by clarifying who is meant by the Spirit and showing how to discover God's will.

In addition, youth leaders should be acquainted with materials that may be used to develop program themes and plans, suggest special-emphasis meetings, or form the basis for small discussion groups of an informal nature. See the bibliography at the end of this book.

STEWARDSHIP OF TIME, TALENT, TREASURE

More and more laymen are saying that the task of the church is their task; more and more young people are thinking of the church as a living, growing, working organism, not an ecclesiastical body that plans and carries out religious activities. They are identifying themselves with the living church.

Many young people are tithing their time. The church needs this time to carry out her full mission, and each young member needs this experience of joyful service. Many young people help in mission projects, conduct street meetings, cottage services, direct missionary bands, teach Sunday school or weekday Bible school, expand the Sunday-school library, plan and conduct junior Sunday evening meetings, or sew for relief.

There is a vast time potential within every youth group.

Personal commitment to the lordship of Christ has an amazing effect on the use of talents of young people. Youth fellowships throughout the Christian church are unearthing abundance of talent. Here are a few ways young people have shared their talents: Erla gave two nights a week to take dictation and type letters for the secretary of a local mission board. Bernard, a sign painter, painted display posters and banners for camps and conferences. John, an accountant, headed the committee to audit the books of the church. Edna's personal interest in crafts led to a craft class for girls. Mary, a nurse, taught first-aid courses to young people of the congregation. Nadine's natural talent to tell stories led her to call together for Bible stories the children of a community who had no Sunday-school privileges. Henry sold religious books one day a week, and through this mission helped lost and troubled souls. Dan, a mechanic, repaired his pastor's car. Clyde, a music teacher, directed the young people's chorus.

Young people often feel that they have little to give in the way of treasure. They are just beginning to earn, and their expenses eat into their incomes. Many are using their earnings to get started in a business, to finance an education, or they may be saving to establish a home or buy a car. Even though they realize that their possessions and gifts are really God's and should be used to His glory, they may hesitate to give a tithe or to budget an offering from their income. Others feel that the giving of treasure should represent not only honest toil, but also love and sacrifice, and they delight in participating in the church's program through their cash gifts.

Enthusiastic leaders can stimulate young people to stewardship of their time by suggesting avenues of service which require little highly specialized talent or great possessions. For example, young women could organize into service teams of two's and give several hours a week to the pastor in tasks he may assign, such as: visiting the sick or shut-ins, delivering promotional literature, calling on those who are indifferent, or in need. Young men likewise could make religious surveys, do chores for someone who is ill, plow the minister's garden, or paint his house. Many young people could serve as boys' and girls' camp counselors.

Most youth leaders know that young people can be encouraged to spend at least one year or more in Christian service. Religious groups who have required this have had astonishing success. And since government conscription has awakened many Christians to the possibilities and power of Christian witness in concentrated effort, hundreds of young people have participated in voluntary service activities. Youth leaders should call attention to the year-round voluntary service opportunities available at home or abroad through the Mennonite Central Committee and the Mennonite Relief and Service Committee. There are open doors in relief, itinerant evangelism, hospitals, and city and rural missions. For those who have only one open summer there are youth teams, colporteur and survey teams, industrial study groups, and teaching missions.

Any youth group wishing to feature voluntary service

possibilities could request slides, speakers, program materials, fliers, information about applications, news of specific openings, and suggestions for programs from the proper service committees.

Every youth leader has unlimited opportunities to awaken young people to the dedication of their talents to the work of the church. It is just as important that the carpenter, the plumber, the plasterer, and the truck driver serve through their skills as it is for the teacher, singer, public speaker, secretary, typist, or printer to do so. The youth leader needs to seek ways to employ the abilities and skills of the youth of the church for the church's welfare, growth, and outreach.

Helping youth to develop a conviction about giving systematically of their treasure is not so easy. Some youth groups have discovered that setting up a budget, based on the planned giving of the members, increases the interest of the young people in contributing as they are financially able. Other groups have tried special projects through which to arouse interest and conviction. These were not based on special earning efforts but on planned giving over a longer period of time. Some groups have discovered that the study of Milo Kauffman's book, *The Challenge of Christian Stewardship,* is a stimulus to thoughtful consideration of the Christian's responsibility to give of his money to the work of the church.

Chapter 5

Guidance for Special Problems

THE WHY AND HOW OF THINKING

MOST PEOPLE are not satisfied to "chust set," as was Mabel Dunham's Nancy of whom it was said, "Sometimes she sets and thinks, but most of the time she 'chust' sets." People want to relive the past, create something new, or solve their problems. They think.

To those who have lived well, thinking of the past is a great source of pleasure. To relive happy experiences is to associate again with people whom we appreciate, and to do again those things we enjoyed. This type of thinking helps us to see the good qualities in others and tends to make us desire to enjoy over again the things that are good. We also are made conscious of our mistakes and the experiences which we regret. We are thinking to an advantage when we desire to avoid a repetition of those errors, by planning to follow more desirable modes of conduct.

Daydreaming is natural among young people and is not necessarily harmful. Only when it takes excessive time that should be given to something more worth while is it questionable.

To create something new demands thought. When the housewife plans a new combination of ingredients and blends flavors to prepare a new dish, she is doing creative thinking. She daydreams also, but in addition she exerts more effort to make her dreams work for her. Combining scientific facts in new ways is creative thinking that often leads to important discoveries. Through this type of thinking roads and bridges are built, effective legislation is initiated, songs are composed, and pictures are painted. Even such a simple thing as the arrangement of furniture in a room involves creative thinking. The pastor in the preparation of his sermon thinks creatively when he studies the Scriptures daily and then allows the Holy Spirit to lead him to the specific passage that will most effectively make the appeal he feels the audience should have. The missionary or businessman thinks creatively when he plans his program of work.

Creative thinking demands effort, first in deciding exactly what the goal should be, and then in planning the best procedure for reaching the goal. These may both be vague, but by picking up one part of a pattern here, and discarding a pattern of thought there, the creative person is finally able to achieve what can be called worth-while products of his efforts.

Another type of thinking is problem solving. Some problems are simple and do not call for very deep thought. Others are rather complex. Young people should discover that a most useful type of thinking they can learn is problem solving. There are two methods commonly used. The one is by trial and error. The other is by a more or less regular technique which requires thinking. The first needs no description. Here are the steps for the latter.

1. *Stating the problem.* In the systematic solution of a problem, the first and most important factor is to be able to understand what there is to solve. By getting down to the heart of the problem and stating it accurately in words the solution is already simplified.

2. *Gathering information.* Individuals can no more solve problems without information than a stonemason can build a wall without stones. It is important to use the information one has, but also to collect all additional pertinent information available. This information must be rated in terms of its reliability. This often means seeking the advice of those who have experience in evaluating the kind of information essential to the solution of the problem.

3. *Listing the solutions.* In spite of information, trying something new is always a leap of faith. The more information there is on hand, the less is the risk in a venture, and the more numerous are the possible solutions. Thus, the third step is to state all possible solutions that could be drawn from the information at hand.

4. *Testing the solutions.* Now the thinker gives each possible solution a fair trial, trying to assess its advantages and disadvantages, evaluating and weighing the evidence for and against it. Thus he can logically decide

whether or not to discard a solution, and finally to choose the solution which seems the most satisfactory from every viewpoint.

5. *Making use of the solution.* Occasionally, when the chosen solution is finally put into practice, it is found unusable. Then the problem solver must begin again, gathering more information, for inadequate or incorrect facts are most likely at fault. However, when the data has been carefully collected and analyzed, and the solution is planned on the basis of this information combined with past experience, it usually works.

Discovering that a solution is satisfactory is not only an achievement for one who thought it through, but it becomes valuable information to others with whom it can be shared. One experience in successful problem solving becomes foundational material for further problem solving, when shared with others faced with similar decisions.

Collecting data for problem solving. A good jury delays a decision for or against a defendant until all the evidence is in. In problem solving it is a mark of growing maturity for the young person to delay his conclusions until he has collected enough data to make a sound conclusion. Data may be secured from a variety of sources, but personal experience is often the source that young people rely on the most. But of this young people must be wary, for they do not have a backlog of varied experiences on which to lean heavily. They must rely heavily on other sources.

Of great value are materials in a library, whether it is the Sunday-school library, or the school or public library. To have a vast store of knowledge opened up to them, young people not skilled in the use of libraries need only ask librarians how to use the card indexes, dictionaries, encyclopedias, yearbooks, almanacs, atlases, periodicals, and indexes.

In addition, the fact seeker may draw on the authority and experience of experts. The young woman who is interested in chemistry for a future vocation would hardly speak to her mathematics teacher, but rather to her uncle employed in a chemical laboratory. A young man interested in foreign missionary service would hardly speak first to the family doctor, but to the secretary of a mission board.

Expert advice on almost every subject—whether vocations, avocations, personality development, or finances—is available in books and magazines which keep abreast of scientific discoveries, technical advancements and improvements, and the most efficient methods. A little research and investigating of the advice of experts may also be of considerable worth. The judgment of any one individual should be compared with that of others who have experience in the same field.

Whether written or oral, it is not wise to accept data that lacks adequate evidence. It is necessary, in gathering data, to consult not only those who know what they are talking about, but also to note under what circumstances they speak or write as they do. An advertiser or salesman will naturally be silent on the weak qualities of his products. To get a comprehensive knowledge of his merchandise it would be necessary to interview his competitors. The human mind and conduct are greatly influenced by prejudice, blind spots, slogans, wishful thinking, sweeping statements, faulty memories—to name just a few blind alleys.

Blind alleys along the way to a proper conclusion. A successful conclusion is not only based on a large bulk of information, but also on wise use of this information. The good thinker will train himself to analyze his materials and check for blind alleys that may be diverting his thinking as he moves toward a conclusion.

One blind alley is to mistake the circumstances for the cause. Because two factors are found in the same setting does not necessarily mean they are related. For example, the three Jones boys excel in arithmetic. Their mother believes that "next to godliness is cleanliness." Does it necessarily follow that since Mother Jones demands cleanliness the Jones boys are specialists in arithmetic? Would all boys whose mothers have this slogan become interested in arithmetic? Hardly. There must be another reason.

Failure to consider all the data can lead to a blind alley. One example of this is when we let all sorts of ready-made thoughts dominate our thinking. Take the old saying, "Preachers' sons are bad." Doubtless some preachers' sons are. But are they all bad? Is it, perhaps, that more is expected of them, that they are more in the public eye, and their every move is registered? A study of *Who's Who in America* may reveal that, in proportion to other men's sons, more ministers' sons are named. It's a temptation to use only data that proves the point we want to emphasize.

Some people never get to the truth in a conclusion,

because they believe what they want to believe, because they want to believe it. They may know that facts prove the opposite, yet refuse to accept them. They have a subconscious feeling that their conclusion is a false one, but the desire to believe what they wish or hope to be true is the stronger. The desire of the public to get something for nothing is so strong that fakers and swindlers do a thriving business. In most instances common sense, and a look at the evidence, would prevent the public from being taken in by schemes that capitalize on wishful thinking.

Mental laziness leads to a blind alley. The first facts should never be taken as final, because they may present only a partial picture, a colored picture, or distorted picture. A good way to safeguard against this danger is to subject such a conclusion to the criticism of some intelligent, fair-minded, informed individual. If the conclusion does not seem sound, it may indicate a need for further study of the problem.

Straight thinking is a priceless gift. It comes to the one who has trained his mind to follow a line of thought clearly and concisely. Cloudy thinking is a curse that befalls the one who allows himself to be influenced without giving mental scrutiny to the issue. Prejudice, the influence of the crowd, and propaganda can keep people from right choices, conclusions, attitudes, and decisions. How may young people learn to defend themselves against these forces? First, by being able to recognize them in themselves, and second by thinking straight.

Thinking straight across prejudice. To form and hold

an opinion without taking time to judge fairly is to be prejudiced. The prejudiced mind picks up its biased opinions either out of its environment or from its own faulty thinking. Full-grown prejudices often develop into delusions. Everyone has likes and dislikes which, in a sense, are positive or negative prejudices. These are not necessarily harmful. But when opinions are not based on truth, they become dangerous.

Frequently, the most deeply rooted prejudices develop during childhood, when the child's developing opinions and impressions are at the mercy of his adult associates and environment. They may become so much a part of the individual that he cannot recognize them as such.

Take, for example, those people who still refuse to allow the words "Sunday school" to describe the Biblical instruction they now tolerate in their church. When the Sunday school was first introduced, it was met with tremendous opposition in many parts of the church. Some said that it was the work of the devil. Others decried it as a new sign of worldliness. And still others felt that the young people of the church would get beyond control through it. So strong was the prejudice that there were schisms. Today, religious instruction is hardly an issue, even in these churches; yet the prejudice remains so strong in the minds of some people that Biblical instruction identical to that received in Sunday school must go by some other name.

The mind that is most likely to escape serious prejudices: seeks for truth above all else, looks for all evidence and all arguments for and against, is willing to change, if necessary, and delays a conclusion until an opinion has been tested.

Thinking straight in the midst of the crowd. Two factors in human behavior have become established: most individuals crave the approval of the group and are influenced by the thinking of the majority. Therefore, thinking contrary to social pressure, especially when that thinking is aligned with the minority, is a real test for the trained mind. The Christian youth in an unchristian environment is often called upon to think straight and meet a real test, not only of mind, but also of character.

To keep himself from being influenced unreasonably, the young person needs to ask himself: even though everybody does it, is the majority right? Is the issue of sufficient importance to incur the disapproval of the group? If the issue involves a truth or an ethical principle, the decision would certainly be that it is of sufficient importance to differ with the group.

Thinking straight in spite of propaganda. Propaganda has come to mean the spread of some opinion or belief without the hearer's immediate recognition of the source or motives behind it. Because its purpose is hidden, it encounters less resistance and thus can become a great power, either for good or for evil. Books, magazines, lectures, leaflets, newspapers, television, and the radio—all are tools of propaganda, a powerful and legitimate means of influencing others. It is probably through its uses during wartime and the unscrupulous methods of advertising that the word has received an unpleasant connotation. Everyone, some time or other, is either wholesomely affected or subtly trapped by it.

Perhaps the best way to meet the propagandist on his own level is to understand his methods. The thinker who would get down to truth, dare not accept a statement just because the book says so. And he dare not believe everything in the daily news, whether it is printed, broadcast, or televised.

He will recognize that a propagandist, whether his motives are justifiable or not, will—

(1) keep on presenting his material systematically and incessantly.

(2) try to avoid arguments, but not admit there is another side to the question, except perhaps in private conversation.

(3) try to connect up his idea with some desire of the group to which he is appealing.

(4) make his statements clear and simple so they can be remembered and easily repeated.

(5) slant the propaganda to some particular group and appeal to some basic urge such as the desire to be attractive or to be loved.

The propagandist who is less scrupulous uses also—

(1) high-sounding technical terms which often, in simple words, would not be very impressive.

(2) sweeping statements such as: "Everyone's doing it, or thinking it, or using it."

(3) words that are weighted with feeling, and appeal to the emotions—freedom, love, peace; or, in the negative—liberal, communist, undemocratic, dictatorial.

(4) extravagant or glittering generalities. For example, a political speaker may profess to be aligned with a "just and holy cause" without sufficiently defining the

nature of the "holy cause." A beer company promises a "sense of refreshed well-being" with every bottle. And a car manufacturer claims his product "steals the scene with a newness all its own."

How to Find a Life Vocation

Christ's own sense of mission, His consciousness of the need of submission to the Father, His concern for the purposeful service of His followers, all indicate divine purpose in human life. Through His teachings, and in the Book of Acts, we see that there is a place of contribution for every person in Christ's kingdom—be he tax collector, seller of purple, fisherman, or centurion.

We can be certain that God wants each of His children to respond to His leading and work with Him. Only as His children fully discern and yield to His daily plan and purpose can they achieve fulfillment and joy in service. Thus God performs in man an act of continuous creation.

Youth frequently ask, "Is everyone called to full-time Christian service?" They desire to contribute to the cause of Christ, even though they are interested in a vocation which is not directly connected with the church. During the Reformation this same question troubled reformers. "Could not the cobbler's life be as acceptable to the Lord as the minister's?" They pondered the problem, even though the church of that day considered holy living to be the special task of monks and priests. The Bible called all believers priests! The Bible said that each person would be judged on the basis of his attitudes and faith, not merely by his vocation.

Two college roommates began careers in their home towns. One opened a religious bookstore; the other accepted a bookkeeping position in a bank. They are both Christian witnesses. Did one have a "call" any more than the other? Christian faith says: "No, God calls everyone to full-time service." Faith is not vital unless it is at the center of life. The ultimate goal of any career is to bring honor and glory to God. The Christian, who maintains a sense of calling whatever his vocation, can bring as many souls into the kingdom of Christ as the minister or missionary; and he can achieve the highest goal of any Christian to bring glory to God.

When Christians forget their primary call, and material success becomes their goal, the temptation is to struggle to advance vocationally in order to improve socially or financially. Success is often at the cost of spiritual progress and service.

There is a magnetic attraction in the lives of individuals who glorify the Christian faith through daily vocational duties. It was said of the late and famed Dr. Kelly, of the Johns Hopkins University, that his first business was to tell men of Christ and his second, to be a successful surgeon. He did both well because he spent much of his valuable time with the Lord and His Word. In building His kingdom, the heavenly Father needs good doctors, farmers, and businessmen—provided they maintain a sense of spiritual calling—as well as good ministers and missionaries.

Aids to finding God's vocational plan. The human mind is highly adaptable. An individual may learn to do many things. The early pioneer tilled the soil, felled trees, cut his son's hair, made his own plow, soled his own shoes, and built his own home. Naturally, he performed some of these tasks with greater ease than others. One vocational field may hold many job possibilities. A young person interested in Spanish could, for example, become a teacher of Spanish, a missionary to Spanish-speaking people, an interpreter, a Spanish language linotype operator, a Spanish proofreader, a writer of Christian literature in Spanish, an English teacher among Spanish people, or a relief worker. A young man interested in the soil could become a soil conservationist, a county agent, an agriculture teacher, a florist, a market gardener, a soil research student, or a nurseryman.

No one can make the decision but the individual involved. But here are requisites to making a decision:

Knowledge about jobs. Occupations are legion, although the average person can think only of about one hundred. Actually, there are more than forty thousand occupations in the United States. In any of the broad categories into which occupations are usually divided there are opportunities for skilled and unskilled persons as well as for executives and professionals.

The *professional* or leadership level requires superior intelligence and long training, for the work is mental rather than physical. In this class also are artists, engineers, lawyers, teachers, doctors, business executives, government officials—about 10 per cent of all workers in the United States.

The *semiprofessional* occupations demand shorter

periods of training, two years usually being sufficient. In this group are found laboratory technicians, dental hygienists, photographers, and draftsmen. Entrance requirements in the training schools for this group are less stringent.

The *skilled* level of occupations calls for a good general education, special training in trade school, or some apprenticeship. Good judgment and native ability also are requisites. Bookkeepers, machinists, electricians, mechanics, engravers, carpenters, and bricklayers—these are among the occupations represented by this group.

The *semiskilled* occupations, requiring little or no training, include jobs such as vegetable and fruit pickers, salesgirls, furniture movers, truck drivers, and redcaps.

In the selection of a vocation it is good to study possible future trends. Here are some of them: occupations involving clerical work are on the up trend. Handwork is on the down trend. New occupations are coming up in engineering, chemistry, physics, government service engineering, construction, public health, and social service. There is a shortage of doctors, dentists, engineers, pharmacists, librarians, teachers, and personnel in all areas of the sciences. It is important to discover whether a field is overcrowded, and how many approximately are engaged in the occupation, and where the largest number of openings are likely to occur.

It is also wise to make a list of the occupations related to the vocation in which one finds an interest. From this list, those which do not appeal can be eliminated. From the remaining ones, a few should be selected for intensive study. Begin by constructing a chart with vertical and horizontal lines. In the vertical column to the left, list the vocations to be studied. In the top horizontal blocks, place such items as: years of training required, duties, demand for workers, possible salary, chances for promotion, geographic area of need, opportunity for service to humanity, capital required to begin, and other significant points of interest. Then gather pertinent information and fill in the blocks.

There are several ways to learn about a vocation. Benjamin Franklin tells how his father took him to see tradesmen at work—joiners, bricklayers, turners, braziers—to help him decide on a vocation. Today this could hardly be done in the same way since some trade work is done on a large scale in conjunction with other work. Many factories are open to visitors, and the person interested in a particular job should explore possibilities for observing workers in that field in operation.

Books, compendiums, pamphlets, and professional periodicals are published in the interest of vocational groups. Librarians are glad to assist patrons in finding the most recent books on occupations. They can direct the inquirer to free literature in a particular field, published by the government and by commercial companies. Even though vocational literature may not answer all questions, it does provide much information to introduce the reader to the field.

Successful workers in the field of interest may be unable to answer all questions; but they can share their knowledge and opinions and a firsthand account of the work.

Perhaps the most effective way to study a vocation is to engage in it as an apprentice for a little while. The would-be doctor can obtain a position as an orderly; the would-be painter can get a summer job with a crew. Many young people spend their summers while students experimenting with different types of work in their field of interest. The experience in the prospective work may fascinate or it may save the young person from a long training period which could end only in failure. Research has shown that those happiest in their vocations are those who have had long training periods. Rushing into a vocation *may* bring a lifetime of unhappiness, but changing jobs to find one that is satisfactory is no disgrace.

Knowledge about aptitudes and interests. Grades earned in high school and college are a clue to aptitudes, and point to vocations that should be avoided. One who has difficulty in reading would hardly consider editorial work; someone who cannot attain accuracy in arithmetic would hardly choose bookkeeping.

Colleges, professional schools, high schools, and many business firms give mental and aptitude tests and provide scientifically designed interest inventories. Human engineering firms administer batteries of tests to those who want further knowledge of their aptitudes, abilities, and skills to help them choose a vocation. These tests enable young persons to discover as objectively as possible just where their chances for success are greatest.

Those who choose work unchallenging to their abilities find themselves disinterested and frustrated. Likewise, those who choose work beyond their ability find themselves constantly under strain. He who serves cheerfully in the area for which he is best fitted, no matter what level, is doing his greatest service to humanity.

A passive interest never leads to real success. The Reidenbachs were shiftless, sluggish farmers. But as the nine sons grew to manhood, each entered a trade that required mechanical skill. Each became prominently successful. They enjoyed their work, and even their father discovered he was more interested in a trade than in being a farmer. But in his youth, the only honorable thing to do was farming; and, unfortunately, he had never considered any other vocation. But he did not force his sons to make the same mistake.

Knowledge about emotional and physical health. After interest and aptitude for a certain occupation have been established, an individual should consider the emotional and physical health demands the vocation makes. These should be checked against his own physical and emotional inventory.

Professional and semiprofessional occupations require endurance of mind and nerve. Medical service demands physical endurance and disciplining of self for rest and recreation, as do masonry, carpentry, and farming, which also call for physical strength. The tendency in jobs where one is self-employed, or free to set his own hours, is to overwork—to the point of neglecting his health. Other jobs impose indoor privations which those who love the out-of-doors cannot endure. Some jobs necessitate working where there are constant noises and vibrations, others where people are coming and going, some permit little association with people. Certain types of work call for personalities that enjoy meeting the public; for example, salesmanship or nursing.

Young people who are not certain about their personality qualities should seek counsel from a high school psychologist, vocational adviser, youth leader, pastor, or trusted friend. They should also take personality tests which high schools and colleges would be able to recommend.

Knowledge about vocations. After they have limited the vocational field by checking their aptitudes, interests, qualifications, and physical and mental health, young people may be inclined to select the vocation that pays the most money. The size of the pay check is an important item in a commercialized economy such as ours—where the average income per family is $4,800, and a railroad conductor can get $6,600, and the janitor may be the best-paid employee in a school.

But the fact remains that some vocations bring rewards that are greater than money. Teachers and personnel directors are sometimes ill-paid, but they have the opportunity to influence thousands of lives, and to guide people into wholesome adjustments to life. Such occupations are stimulating to their intellectual development, as well.

Some of the finest rewards come to those who choose a lifework through which they can express their innermost selves. When the architect plans a building, the artist paints a picture, the landscape gardener plans a garden, the author writes a book, or the musician composes a song, each receives pleasure in giving to the world what he considers his own and best creation.

A wall that was laid by Haas Welton had prestige. Men hired him to lay walls, not only because his work spelled durability, but also because there was a unique beauty in every Welton wall. They were landmarks. Haas Welton had learned that money is not the key to happiness; but happiness lies in the consciousness that others value our work, and that we are doing it as unto God. This true secret of happiness through service to his fellow men had become a way of life to Welton.

The word vocation means a calling, or summons, and in olden days the work of a man was so inextricably associated with the man that he was often named by the service he performed to humanity. Simon was a tanner, Lydia a seller of purple, Peter a fisherman, Joseph a carpenter. Present-day family names can sometimes be traced to an ancestor who was, for example, a weaver, a baker, a driver, a smith, a shoemaker, a painter, or a butcher. And today, nicknames are often given to people because of their keen interest in their vocation or a hobby. The nickname attachment is not so important, but it illustrates the wholeness of personality that one can see where the person and job are well mated. One is wise to choose a vocation that offers more than monetary rewards. But when a person's sole reason for a particular vocational choice is money, it ceases to be a vocation and becomes a job.

"I have come," said a factory worker to his employer, "to ask you to help me solve a problem. For twelve years I have gone in and out your factory doors. Now

I am conscious that I have just been doing a job. I am not happy and not fitted for the work I do. What can I do about it?"

What could the factory hand do? It would be much more difficult at this point to move into the vocation he desired. The work he thought he would now like for a vocation, and for which he discovered an aptitude, called for several years of training. He had a family to support, no funds to see him through a training period, and half of his best earning years already lived. Money had led him to take the job in the first place, but it hadn't filled a basic need God has put into every individual: the need to feel he is performing his best service for humanity, through the combination of aptitudes, interests, and personality that are uniquely his.

Knowledge of God's will. Vocational possibilities should be judged in the light of the Scriptures. All genuinely born-again Christians are at heart soul winners. Spiritual influence, by life and word, is a natural expression of a vital Christian. Whenever the Christian enters a work that day after day vexes and sorely tries his Christian spirit, he is treading on dangerous ground. Although he is sent to be a light to the world, he is not expected to work in places where his testimony is not accepted. In such an atmosphere lived the ancient Lot. Jesus advised His true disciples to shake the dust off their feet against such a work and such an environment.

The Scriptures advocate the fellowship of saints for mutual spiritual growth. When work takes an individual away from Christian contacts, that individual must seek to win others into the kingdom or lose his vital fellowship. History indicates that totally isolated Christians either testified and lived, or kept silent and were swallowed up by the world. At no time does a vocation justify the loss of church contact.

A Christian should choose a vocation that builds lives rather than destroys them. Careers in the Army and Navy are hardly suitable vocations for those who believe that Christ's kingdom is not of this world—otherwise His followers would fight. In this class also are industries whose main contracts are for government armament or military expansion programs. Work that saves lives morally, mentally, and spiritually—that builds character, that leaves a legacy to humanity in thought and exemplary living, that constructs rather than destroys—fills a vital human need and meets the requirements of the Scriptures.

When a young person dedicates his life to the Lord, the Holy Spirit can lead him. God's Spirit makes no mistakes in the lives of those who want to do the Father's will. Those who turn their futures over to the guidance of the Spirit have inner peace, and life becomes a holy adventure. They are free from the strain and worry and fear that often accompany the choice and apprenticeship of a career. To know God is to follow His will day by day.

The ultimate and final decision for a vocation must be made by the individual, and this decision and dedication cannot be made without submitting the whole in prayer. Prayer will not bring the answer when there are mixed motives of service. Prayer will not answer

10

the questions in a final examination for one who has not studied hard in the course. Prayer will not give information about the world of jobs and needs. But when individuals have done their part, prayer can become the final touchstone of decision. The young person can quietly and honestly lay the whole matter before the Lord. There will probably be no angelic visitant or striking vision. But as the Christian prays, there comes into his consciousness an increasing clearness as to what the will of the Lord is. This becomes a stronger and stronger impression until, as an impelling force, it gives birth to a conviction. No Christian can expect to arrive at his decision in exactly the same way as another. But having gathered all the facts, he can in faith trust God to lead into the right vocation.

HEARING THE CALL OF A CHURCH VOCATION

The church has full-time work for those who have courage, are willing to work, and have ability to solve hard problems. She does not offer large salaries nor opportunities for great financial advancement. She may even ask the surrender of the comforts of home and the close contact of friends. The young person who enlists under the banner of Christ will have little time for himself. If he is a leader, he may be lonely and yet be surrounded by those who need him.

For full-time service, the church needs the best type of youth she can find. She requires the highest type of character, the most deeply equipped spiritually, the most talented, the best prepared. Her diversified program makes great demands of each individual. Especially is this true in her foreign program. Each service area has specified qualifications for its candidates, but these six general qualities are essential to all who would enter the service of the church.

1. *A definite experience and assurance of salvation.* Only those with a message from the heart—a testimony of experience rather than the testimony of knowledge— can expect to win souls. With this quality should be linked the desire and ability to draw food from the Word, as well as to fellowship with God in prayer, and to sense the guidance of the Holy Spirit.

2. *A genuine love for souls.* Whether missionary, editor, teacher, or laborer, the church institutional worker's greatest business should be to bring lives to Christ. He should not permit routine to monopolize his time and thought. He should recognize every individual as a soul to be saved or strengthened, or as one with whom he may have Christian fellowship.

3. *A consciousness of divine commission.* He should be able to say: "This is the will of God; this is my place." Aware of being under divine command, he should be careful to fully respect others who also serve the Master, but whose service differs. Loyalty to the church is very essential but pride of church may prove a dangerous peril.

4. *Humility, the foundation for adaptability.* Humility should be the most desired quality of a Christian worker. Yet it is perhaps the least achieved. Humbleness makes a person willing to learn from others and to be open-minded toward his own faults. A humble person studies the techniques of tact. Christian workers

often live and work in close and constant contact. Humility oils the irritations and gives the death blow to a dogmatic and domineering attitude. It helps a worker to be a follower as well as a leader.

5. *Qualities of character.* Conscientiousness makes an individual faithful in details. A sense of responsibility helps him be alert for tasks to be done and to apply himself with the efficiency required to accomplish them with dispatch. Patience helps him accept delays. Common sense makes him logical and reasonable about everyday things. A sense of humor removes the sting from awkward or hopeless situations. Poise permits him to relax, and at the same time keep his mind alert. A servant of the Lord must avoid extremes—fanatical movements, changes by revolution, or deadly passivity. His zeal must be tempered with wisdom, his piety with strength of character.

6. *Thorough preparation for the work to which God has called.* He who hears a call to service must hear also a call to preparation for that service. Dedication may involve as much diligent study and concentration of energies for learning as would preparation for any other career. Serving the church is not an easy way to a position of authority or acclaim. Training is as essential to becoming a foreign missionary as it is to becoming a dietitian or a public school teacher.

Kinds of Church Vocations. There are various groupings of church vocations, each of which includes a variety of different tasks.

Ministerial. Besides pastors for self-supporting congregations, ministers are needed for itinerant evangelism and other positions. Slum dwellers, Puerto Rican tomato pickers, Mexican beet thinners, Indians of the Chaco, jungle farmers of Africa, rice growers of India, tea gatherers of Japan are examples of neglected people who need to hear the Gospel. There are large new suburban residential centers in expanding cities that have few or no churches. Many rural church doors are closed for want of pastors, and many rural areas have never had churches. Chaplains are needed for hospitals, prisons, industrial organizations. These are but sample suggestions. And although the church does not ordain women to the ministry, many open doors mentioned here are also calls to women with an evangelistic vision.

Missionary. There is no stereotyped person to be cited as an example of the kind God calls as a missionary. Here, as in the ministry, He uses a variety of interests, training, and talent. Besides missionaries who are pastors and evangelists, He uses station superintendents, doctors, nurses, technicians, dietitians, secretary-bookkeepers, home department workers, linguists, youth leaders, builders, colporteurs, directors of women's work, translators, educational directors, mechanics, and industrial missionaries. Teachers are needed for mission schools, for language training centers, and for schools for missionary children. There must also be missionary rest and retirement homes and those who can care for them.

Educational. As the educational program of the church expands, the demand increases for professionally trained and spiritually equipped teachers for seminaries, colleges, nurses' training schools, high schools, and Christian day schools. Schools need administrators, counselors, nurses, secretaries, bookkeepers, librarians, dietitians, field representatives, financiers, public relations personnel, directors of alumni interests and activities, planners of promotional material—to mention only a few. Consecrated persons are also needed to fill such jobs as chefs, housekeepers, matrons, supervisors of grounds, and maintenance men.

Literature. Closely allied to education, and truly educational in itself, is publication of literature. A constant stream of capable, efficient, and spiritually minded persons is needed to educate and inform the church and reach the world through the printed page. This corps of workers includes editors, their assistants and writers. More writers are needed for books, as well as for articles and stories for periodicals and magazines. Curriculum writers are needed for materials for Sunday-school, weekday Bible school, summer Bible school, and youth program plans. Also needed are artists, photographers, colporteurs, bookstore managers, clerks, printers, pressmen, offset specialists, linotype operators, proofreaders, bookbinders, mailing clerks, machine operators, shipping clerks, information clerks, bookkeepers, secretaries, and typists. The opportunities are varied.

Institutional. Opportunities for a church vocation through institutions are being constantly increased. Hospitals, both general and mental, homes for the aged and convalescing, child welfare programs, both through private homes and planned villages, seek Christian youth as helpers. Doctors, psychiatrists, registered nurses, superintendents, social case workers, recreational and craft directors, physiotherapists, technicians, and dietitians are needed. Practical nurses, nurse aides, orderlies, chefs, laundresses, farmers, gardeners, matrons, and truck drivers are merely a suggestive few of those needed to perform the complete task of these institutions.

How God calls. Sometimes young people feel that they need not consider a church vocation unless they are called through some miraculous experience. Yet most of the capable, Spirit-filled persons who have found a vocation within the church testify that theirs was a call through a steadily growing and quietly nurtured faith. God works through ordinary circumstances as well as through extraordinary. In the early church thousands were added daily to the church, and they went everywhere preaching the Word; yet we have the record of only a few who had an unusual call. What then should a young person consider a call to a church vocation?

Is a conviction a call? God stakes a claim in every life. Some live in a twilight consciousness of this claim for a long time and then gradually realize that God is calling them. Conviction may be confused with impulse or desire in the matter of type and place of service. God called John to the ministry. He had convictions, he said, for mass evangelism, yet all who knew him felt his power lay in his pen. God closed the door to evangelism and opened the door for writing. Conviction alone is not a call.

Is a church invitation a call? Young people who offer their lives to the church may be confronted with more than one opportunity, and they may be capable of filling any of them. Of itself, an invitation from the church is not likely to be sufficient evidence of God's leading to be reassuring when the real tests come on the battle-front of service.

Is need a call? Conviction is born of knowledge. First impressions to enter the work of the church may come when an individual hears of a need somewhere. Vast frontiers of need have never been touched by the church and others remain undeveloped. Knowledge of need may feed the flames of conviction and give a sense of direction; but need alone does not constitute a call.

Is preparedness a call? A small congregation needed a pastor. Henry, in a neighboring congregation, had all the formal training necessary. He was spiritually equipped for the task. He began as a filler-in, and the ministerial committee hoped he might become the permanent pastor. But time proved he did not have the leadership ability needed for that particular congregation. Preparedness alone is not a call to the work of the church.

The Holy Spirit calls those within hearing distance through a combination of circumstances. The call to a church vocation may be distinguished from other vocational calls as a summons to the special task of serving the church. A person is being called when he realizes either gradually or suddenly that:

1. the most important task of the Christian is to lead others to take Christ into their lives.

2. the greatest and most worthy cause to which a life can be dedicated is the church and kingdom work.

3. though unworthy, he possesses qualifications essential to a church vocation.

How to Live Victoriously

To many young people, Christian faith seems to have a "missing link." They know that God promises victory, but they do not know how to receive it. They believe in Christ as Saviour and guide, but they do not understand Him as life and power. They have experienced that faith in Christ does not produce perfection, and they cannot believe that it is possible to be sinless, because they have not known personal victory.

They may express their feelings in words similar to these:

"I have tried and tried to be like Christ, but I always fail."

"Last week I yielded my life to Christ, but I just can't control my temper."

"Joe can pray all right, but you ought to hear his language among the fellows."

What is victory?

1. *Victory is appropriating resurrection power.* The Holy Spirit does dwell within every Christian. Paul wrote to the Corinthians: "What? Know ye not that your body is the temple of the Holy Ghost which is in you" (I Corinthians 6:19)? The Holy Spirit is God with us. Paul also wrote to the Ephesians that he was praying that they might know "what is the exceeding greatness of his power to us-ward who believe, according to the working of his mighty power, which he wrought in Christ, when he raised him from the dead, and set him

11

at his own right hand in the heavenly places" (Ephesians 1:19, 20). What a staggering thought for the youth who believe it!

"How shall we acquire this power?" young people ask. The secret lies in one small verb, yield. Yielding to the Holy Spirit means giving in and abandoning self. "Yield yourselves unto God, as those that are alive from the dead, and your members as instruments of righteousness unto God" (Romans 6:13). It is not trying and trying to be like Christ that brings victory, but yielding and yielding to the Holy Spirit, who is Christ working within us. This is not magic, but the mysterious work of God's goodness (grace).

2. *Victory is making decisions and forming habits for righteousness.* Salvation does not bring immediate glorified perfection. Young people whose lives have been controlled by evil habits will have to learn by the help of the Spirit to break these evil habits. This is not easy, for it involves the exercise of the will; and human nature is always human. The "babe in Christ" is certain to stumble while he is learning to walk. It is a matter of applying the truth of Romans 6:13. "Yield yourselves unto God . . . and your members as instruments of righteousness unto God." The hand that had reached out to steal will now reach out to serve in the name of Christ. The tongue that lied will testify for Christ. The eye that enjoyed lustful stimuli will now be used to read the Bible. It is an experience of rightabout-face. According to Galatians 2:20 it is "not I, but Christ," who forgives when cheated, who keeps calm when the tractor breaks down, who smiles when the cake will not rise.

To feel the bitterness and not express it, or to think the evil and not commit it, is not victory. True victory is in the heart. Inner victory is proved by controlled conduct.

Victory implies that the whole of life is involved in righteous living. "But like as he who called you is holy, be ye yourselves also holy in all manner of living" (I Peter 1:15, ASV).

3. Victory is triumph in the hour of deepest trial. The temptations of Satan are many and varied. He knows in what area each person is vulnerable. The impulsive person may be tempted to act before thinking—to commit an overt sinful act. Others may be tempted by the more subtle and deep sins of the mind, such as pride, passion, envy, or jealousy. But over all these temptations, Christ offers victory. Here are some suggestions for appropriating His power:

Fill the memory library with Scripture. The Spirit can bring to memory the right Scripture only if it has been memorized. Nothing is so potent in the time of crisis as the Word. Satan has no answer for it and is therefore defeated. Jesus used this method in His own triumph.

Do not debate the temptation. The devil is crafty and knows how to appeal to people. Showing any interest in Satan's suggestions gives him a foothold, and then if one follows his lures, the victory rapidly becomes his. "Submit yourselves therefore to God. Resist the devil, and he will flee from you" (James 4:7). Satan fears the Christian who is yielded to God.

Be assured that no temptation is too great for victory.

"There hath no temptation taken you but such as is common to man: but God is faithful, who will not suffer you to be tempted above that ye are able; but will with the temptation also make a way to escape, that ye may be able to bear it" (I Corinthians 10:13). The way of escape is in yielding to the voice of the Spirit in each little decision instead of yielding to self or Satan.

Testify of victory, and help others resist temptation. Satan dislikes the Christian's testimony of victory because it gives others courage; and that means less victories for him. Share victories, but beware of boasting and glorying in self. Come to the rescue of others facing the hour of trial or defeat. "Brethren, if a man be overtaken in a fault, ye which are spiritual, restore such an one in the spirit of meekness; considering thyself, lest thou also be tempted" (Galatians 6:1).

Take refuge in prayer. The Christian may go boldly to God, for Christ is there to take your petition to the Father. Jesus Himself was tempted in every way that we are, but He was victorious. And because He had victory, we, too, may have victory, by asking for power to overcome. "For in that he himself hath suffered being tempted, he is able to succour them that are tempted" (Hebrews 2:18). "Let us therefore come boldly unto the throne of grace, that we may obtain mercy, and find grace to help in time of need."

Christ prays to the Father for our victory. "It is Christ that died, yea rather, that is risen again, who is even at the right hand of God, who also maketh intercession for us" (Romans 8:34). Paul also speaks of the Spirit helping us. "For we know not what we should pray for as we ought: but the Spirit itself maketh intercession for us with groanings which cannot be uttered" (Romans 8:26).

4. *Victory is being able to differentiate between temptation and sin.* The Scripture says, "As he thinketh in his heart, so is he" (Proverbs 23:7). Temptation has become sin only if the evil thought is accepted and entertained and ultimately leads to a sinful act. The thought that is examined and rejected is not sin. Man is what he thinks; but when he rejects evil he has accepted righteousness and has victory.

5. *Victory is knowing what to do with sin.* If Satan breaks through the barrier of the Christ-man fellowship, what procedure should a young person take to get right with God? Seeking pardon at once restores fellowship and restrains the tendency to stray deeper into sin. Questions young people ask about sin are:

How can I find forgiveness and enjoy fellowship again? The Apostle John reassured Christians who wondered whether God's love was operative when they sinned. John said: "If we confess our sins, he is faithful and just to forgive us our sins, and to cleanse us from all unrighteousness" (I John 1:9). God grants forgiveness as soon as man confesses and forsakes sin.

Harboring unconfessed sin calls a halt to spiritual advances. It becomes a hindrance to Christian growth and service. Gossip, jealousy, hatred, deceit, or any sin of the mind, heart, or hand can do the evil work.

To whom must confession be made? Certainly confession must be made to God, since all sin draws the clouds of disfavor between God and man. Not until man seeks forgiveness through Christ can the cloud be removed and fellowship continued.

The Scriptures do not say specifically to which individuals confession shall be made. Practices differ in various church communities and certainly the one who has transgressed should not do less than confess to those wronged. The one, or ones, wronged should be told that the penitent desires forgiveness. And who but the one who has offended should make this confession and restore property or good will?

What sins must be confessed? The Scripture does not say, "If we confess our little sins," or "if we confess our big sins" we shall be forgiven. It says, "our sins." All sin must be confessed to God. It might seem unlikely that others could profit by hearing the confession of sins that affect only the individual and God, unless, perhaps, the Holy Spirit would demand this of the sinner. James 5:16 says: "Confess your faults one to another, and pray one for another, that ye may be healed." And the sin may not be as personal as the individual may suppose. Someone else might be encouraged to seek the joy of forgiveness, when he hears the confession of another person.

How often must sin be confessed? Confession means forgiveness in God's sight. If a person cannot feel forgiveness after he has confessed, it may be that he has not confessed completely or perhaps he is being tempted to confusion by Satan. But one must remember it is the fact and not the feeling that makes forgiveness a settled matter between God and man.

Sometimes it is difficult for youth to forgive themselves for their mistakes and sins, so they chastise themselves with guilt feelings, believing that they cannot be forgiven unless they suffer some punishment. This is spirit destroying and not according to the Scriptures. Christ accepts the sinner when he come repenting. He accepts the Christian when he comes confessing. He forgives. When the Christian confesses his mistakes and sins, he must accept forgiveness and use the experience as a steppingstone to victory and achievement.

6. *Victory is made continuous by abiding in Christ.* When young people have experienced defeat, and then found the way of victory, they frequently fear they will again lose this glorious privilege in Christ. If Christians desire more than anything else in the world to do the will of God, there is no reason why Jesus' promises will not be fulfilled in their lives. He has said:

"He that abideth in me, and I in him, the same bringeth forth much fruit: for without me ye can do nothing" (John 15:5).

"If ye abide in me, and my words abide in you, ye shall ask what ye will, and it shall be done unto you" (John 15:7).

However, one disobedience to the known will of God, or one act of grieving the Spirit, may mar this oneness with Christ. But always, when the Christian comes in confession, he receives forgiveness and may continue to abide in Christ.

It is futile to seek victory for the next year and the next. The Christian does not need victory that far in the future. Abiding is a moment by moment process. Victory, too, is moment by moment.

7. *Victory is recognizing the Spirit's leading.* Young Christians frequently do not understand truths about the Spirit, and they therefore cannot recognize His voice. Unless it is explained, they may not understand that "Christ in you" is the same as the indwelling Spirit, or the Holy Spirit within, or the abiding Presence of Christ. Other names for the Holy Spirit are the Comforter, the Spirit of God, the Spirit of Glory, the Spirit of Life, the Spirit of Truth, the Spirit of Grace, and the Spirit of Promise. The Bible also speaks of God working in the believer.

Young people must learn to recognize the voice of the Spirit, just as sheep learn the voice of the shepherd, by following him. As young people obey what they do know to be God's will as revealed in the Bible, their acquaintance with Him is increased, and they can learn to recognize His mind and will in other matters. They are hearing His voice. Until they are able to recognize the voice of the Spirit with certainty, they should be willing, in times of doubt, to seek the advice of others who have experienced His leadership.

In adolescence, impulses lie close to the surface of general conduct. For this reason it is often difficult for adolescents to differentiate between impulses and the Spirit's leading. God uses man's impulses to carry out His will in the lives of His children; but Satan also uses the impulsive part of people's nature, especially of youth. In order to discover whether the Holy Spirit is the source of a conviction, young people must first desire to do God's will when they do discover it, and then submit their conviction to the following tests.

Does this leading conform to the teaching of the Bible? The Bible and God's Spirit are not contradictory for God is never divided against Himself. The Bible is clear on a great many details, more than most Christians recognize. Those matters that are not explicit must be decided by other points of this test.

Do providential circumstances give evidence that this is a true lead? The Spirit never leads in a direction where He will not go before and open the way. If the way is not open, the voice must be other than the true Shepherd's.

Do inner faculties, enlightened by the Spirit of God, consent to the lead? God expects individuals to use the judgment and common sense He has given them to ascertain His will in carrying out everyday affairs.

Does the deep, inner impression persist? Sometimes, when the lead has not passed the two tests above, the impression still persists. Then it may be wise to wait until the guidance is clear without question.

Sometimes young people deal carelessly with the Spirit, and in this way they lose the precious consciousness that once meant so much to them. The Spirit may withdraw the consciousness of His presence for these reasons:

He is grieved. Foolish talking, jesting, sacrilegious comments, busyness with everyday affairs, and neglect of meditation and Bible reading and prayer tend to cause the Holy Spirit to be grieved.

He is quenched. The Spirit prompts the child of God to make choices for righteousness. When this moment by moment prompting is ignored, and youth take their own way, the Spirit cannot keep their hearts sensitive to His will.

It is also the work of the Spirit to testify of Christ through the believer. If young people fail to testify when prompted, the Spirit cannot do His work.

Furthermore, it is the work of the Spirit to make holy the life of the believer. When young Christians refuse to get rid of sin, no matter how small, or are unwilling to yield their wills, the Spirit is frustrated.

He is lied to. Sometimes parents, youth leaders, pastors, and evangelists are responsible for the circumstances forcing young people to make premature statements of consecration, implying that they have surrendered all when actually there has been no inner decision. They may know in their hearts that what they agree to is not sincere, but because nearly everyone else present makes a similar commitment, they yield to social pressure and thereby lie to the Spirit. This is unfortunate, for it results in defeat. Unless there is a real heart yielding, merely to profess at a consecration service can mean nothing more than the emotional act of following the crowd. This, of course, leaves the young Christian less able to respond to the voice of the Spirit when He speaks personally.

The Spirit has silent times. He does not withdraw, but He does not always make Himself known or felt. Even the most yielded believer may experience this. In times such as this, youth must rely on God's faithfulness to keep His promises. He must enter into new ventures of faith.

A Bibliography

FOR LEADERS OF YOUNG PEOPLE

Clarice M. Bowman, *Ways Youth Learn* (Harper, 1952). Excellent on ways of challenging and presenting the Christian faith to young people.

Rollo May, *The Art of Counselling* (Abingdon, 1939). A helpful book for ready reference when the counselor needs to refresh his memory before a series of interviews.

H. S. Elliot, *Group Discussion in Religious Education* (Association Press, 1946). Inexpensive (50¢) help on making the discussion method effective.

Arnold Gesell (and others), *Youth: The Years from Ten to Sixteen* (Harper, 1957). Findings of scientific studies in understandable language, with suggestions for the direction of youth's energies toward self-development and maturity.

G. Haglund and V. Grabill, *Youth Leaders' Handbook* (Zondervan, 1958). True to its title. An unusually good manual and written from a definitely evangelical viewpoint. A real "How To" book for youth workers.

Grace Sloan Overton, *Living with Parents* (Broadman, 1954). A well-known youth counselor discusses problems of growing up such as interest in dating, vocations, homemaking and religion.

Dorothy M. Roberts, *Leadership of Teen-Age Groups* (Association Press, 1950). Covers the world of the teen-ager, how to organize meaningful activity, and program planning.

Henry N. Tani, *Ventures in Youth Work* (Christian Education Press, 1957). Eleven chapters written by an active director of youth work. Recommended because it is recent, has an excellent style, the viewpoint is Christian, and lists bibliography, films, and agencies.

Claude F. Boyer, *Counseling Youth* (Faith and Life Press, 1959). A pamphlet and helpful guide for adult counselors in local youth work.

Rudolph M. Wittenberg, *How to Help People* (Association Press, 1953). A very readable handbook dealing with questions that young people have, of particular help to adults who counsel with young people.

Evelyn M. Duvall, *Keeping Up with Teen-agers*. Public Affairs Pamphlet. No. 127 (22 East 38th St., New York 16, N.Y.). A sprightly presentation of the changing teen-ager to assure parents and youth workers they can keep abreast of youth's changes. Inexpensive.

Rinker, Rosiland, *The Years That Count* (Zondervan, 1958). A straightforward I-to-you discussion of education, courtship, and choosing a vocation for youth. Calls young people to discover whether they are Christians by persuasion, association, or conviction. Makes the Christian life relevant to youth.

COURTSHIP AND MARRIAGE

H. Clair Amstutz, M.D., *Growing Up to Love* (Herald Press, 1956). Written as a guide for parents to use in planting proper attitudes on the subject of sex.

Evelyn M. Duvall, *Facts of Life and Love for Teenagers* (Association Press, Revised 1956). Of specific help for maturing young people who want to know the biological facts of l.fe.

Public Affairs Pamphlets (22 East 38th St., New York 16, N.Y.). Ralph G. Eckert, *So You Think It's Love*. (No. 161). Lester A. Kirkendall, *Too Young to Marry*. (No. 236). Algermond D. Black, *If I Marry Outside My Religion*. (No. 204).

Esther E. Glass, *When You Date* (Herald Press, 1952). A helpful discussion to young people who are beginning to enter the courtship stage.

James A. Pike, *If You Marry Outside Your Faith* (Harper, 1954). States the implications of marriage outside of the faith and clears some misconceptions.

Henry Bowman, *Marriage for Moderns* (Whittlesey, by McGraw-Hill, 1954). Here are frank answers to personal and intimate questions that young people, getting ready for marriage, or looking forward to it, frequently ask about dating, engagement, marriage and adjustments after marriage. Dr. Bowman is widely known for his sensible approach to these problems.

David R. Mace, *Success in Marriage* (Abingdon, 1958). Into this book the author has packed a great amount of wisdom and understanding about the hazards of marriage and what makes for success in this most rewarding or frustrating of human relationships.

Evelyn M. Duvall and Reuben Hill, *When You Marry* (Association Press, 1947; Revised, 1953). Written in a lively personal style, this book deals with everything that leads up to, prepares for, and pertains to courtship, marriage, and parenthood. Touched with humor and illustrated with line drawings.

Ernest E. Lott, *Christian Youth and Dating* (Good News Broadcasting Association, 1955). Pamphlet. Stresses the idea of honoring Christ in all phases and activities of our life. Good suggestions in positive as well as negative form.

William E. Hulme, *God, Sex and Youth* (Prentice-Hall, 1959). A Scriptural and spiritually sound approach to this problem area. A good discussion of what love should mean in boy-girl relationships.

Vocation

Erma P. Ferrari, *Careers for You* (Abingdon, 1953). A thorough delving into the possibilities, requirements, potentialities of many job areas. Many youth workers will want to be acquainted with this volume for ready reference.

Good Housekeeping's Guide to Successful Homemaking. A practical book of advice from the experience of noted counselors. Deals with problems of adjustment, such as the working wife, when to start a family, and principles of finance.

G. Curtis Jones, *What Are You Doing* (Bethany Press, 1956). Forty portraits of well-known American lay people who are living witnesses to the importance of the Christian attitude in their own lives.

Albert P. Klausler, *Christ and Your Job* (Concordia, 1956). This book is an effort to stimulate and challenge Christians in this day when so many are succumbing to the feeling of futility and are thoroughly unhappy in their jobs. For young people facing the choice of vocation, those who do or should counsel youth, and those unhappy in their job.

Alexander Miller, *Christian Faith and My Job* (Association Press, 1946). Relates the Christian faith to work in our present highly industrialized age. Shows good understanding of the problems of city people.

T. Otto Nall and Bert H. Davis, *Young Christians at Work* (Association Press, 1949). This book shows clearly that every job presents opportunities for a Christian witness.

Harry and Bonaro Overstreet, *The Mind Alive* (Norton, 1954). The nature of emotional well-being and how to attain it. Not distinctively Christian in viewpoint, but helpful to a mature person or counselor.

Walter Reiss, *Teen-Ager, Christ Is for You* (Concordia, 1957). A brief forceful booklet for the unconvinced teen-ager who has not thought about the necessity for decision or who has doubts as to the right one.

Ruth Strang, *The Adolescent Views Himself* (McGraw-Hill, 1957). A readable psychology of adolescence illustrated by a teen-ager, with many discerning paragraphs written by teen-agers themselves.

Special Problems

William E. Hulme, *Face Your Life with Confidence* (Prentice Hall, 1953). A book of case studies and practical psychological advice for all manner of youth problems.

G. Curtis Jones, *Youth Deserves to Know* (Macmillan, 1958). Valuable guide to middle adolescents facing problems and decisions. Treats marriage, work, honesty, freedom, and human relations.

Fritz Kunkel, *My Dear Ego* (Pilgrim Press, 1947). Spiced with humor, this book for adolescents will help them understand how their ideas, hopes, desires, and fears affect their development and mental health.

J. Roswell Gallagher, and Herbert I. Harris, *Emotional Problems of Adolescents* (Oxford University Press, 1958). A guide to help parents, teachers, ministers, and others to understand normal adolescents and their everyday problems. Written by a psychiatrist and physician.

Leslie D. Weatherhead, *Prescription for Anxiety* (Hodder and Stoughton, London, 1956). A practical book to bring courage, hope, and resolution to the deeply troubled. Gives guidance to confused persons, and aids a youth leader to provide sympathetic understanding.

T. B. Maston, *Right or Wrong* (Broadman, 1955). Facts on both sides of many ethical problems that plague youth. Problems include: dancing, petting, drinking, smoking, movies, and others.

Haskell M. Miller, *Understanding and Preventing Juvenile Delin-*

quency (Abingdon, 1958). A well-written and informative book, practical for parents and those who work with youth. Treats the entire scope of juvenile delinquency.

Guy L. Roberts, *How the Church Can Help Where Delinquency Begins* (John Knox, 1958). The author believes the church is better equipped to accomplish something in this area than any other agency. He presents a strong challenge to the church to minister to the troubled souls of delinquent children.

Lance Webb, *Discovering Love* (Abingdon, 1959). Points up the differences between "giving love" and "desiring love." Gives many practical suggestions for putting "giving love" into daily relationships with other people.

RESOURCE AND STUDY MATERIALS

Youth Program Ideas. Volume 1 (1956), Volume 2 (1957), Volume 3 (1957), Volume 4 (1959). (Herald Press, Scottdale, Pa.).

Each volume contains 12 chapters written by specialists in the field. They are designed to give ideas for worship, programs, activity, and their problem-solving situations. They are created for youth, their officers, committee members, advisers, and pastors interested in the local church's program for young people.

Getting Acquainted with the New Testament (Herald Press, 1956).

Introduces the student to the outline, structure, and purpose of the New Testament. Each lesson has a section on Christian life and conduct that endeavors to lead the student to a Biblical approach to personal problems. Intended for grade IX.

Getting Acquainted with the Old Testament (Herald Press, 1956).

Provides the student with a bird's-eye view of the Hebrew people through the Old Testament. Each lesson contains a section on worship and life in the church. Intended for grade X.

Walter Riess, *Teen-ager, The Bible Speaks to You* (Concordia, 1959). This little book could well be the stimulus to start the teen-ager toward meaningful devotional experiences. Forty-three Scripture passages are introduced by youth who tell what the passage has meant in their life.

J. Oswald Sanders, *A Spiritual Clinic* (Moody, 1958). Deals with the problems of Christian experience and Christian service. Contains a wealth of readable and very practical help for counseling or sermon talk preparation. Can be used by everyone including older teen-agers.

Robert McAfee Brown, *The Bible Speaks to You* (Westminster, 1955). An able attempt to put Biblical theology and doctrinal terminology in concepts and language for youth. Always interesting and never superficial.

Donald B. Aldrich, Ed., *The Golden Book of Prayer* (Grosset, 1949). A paperback anthology of prayer for meditation, penitence, thanksgiving, everyday activities, praise, intercession, guidance.

Mary W. Tileston, *Prayers, Ancient and Modern* (Grosset, 1928). A compact book of the choicest prayers of saints of all ages, one for each day of the year. Nicely indexed as to subjects and authors.

William Kramer, *Teen-Agers Pray* (Concordia, 1955). Contains 75 prayers written by youth and for young people on concerns of interest to them.

Milo Kauffman, *The Challenge of Christian Stewardship* (Herald Press, 1955). A helpful source book for ideas and insights on stewardship of money. Useful for teaching.

Ruth Schroeder, *Youth Programs for Christian Growth* (Abingdon, 1957). Contains 32 complete worship programs built around (1) basic Christian beliefs and (2) growth in Christian discipleship.

Oliver Cummings, *The Youth Fellowship* (Judson, 1956). Contains ten chapters filled with very practical help on making the church vital for youth.

Howard W. Ellis, *Evangelism for Teen-Agers* (Abingdon, 1958). Written for senior young people about how they can evangelize other youth for Christ and the church.

Christian Fellowship (Faith and Life Press, 1959). Pamphlet that provides help for fellowship committees in local youth groups.

MYF Handbook. Official Guide for Mennonite Youth Fellowship (Mennonite Publishing House, 1957).

Singing Together (Herald Press, 1950). Contains 96 selections for various occasions.